Learning
TO WORK

Learning TO WORK

The Case for Reintegrating Job Training and Education

W. NORTON GRUBB

Russell Sage Foundation · New York

The Russell Sage Foundation

The Russell Sage Foundation, one of the oldest of America's general purpose foundations, was established in 1907 by Mrs. Margaret Olivia Sage for "the improvement of social and living conditions in the United States." The Foundation seeks to fulfill this mandate by fostering the development and dissemination of knowledge about the country's political, social, and economic problems. While the Foundation endeavors to assure the accuracy and objectivity of each book it publishes, the conclusions and interpretations in Russell Sage Foundation publications are those of the authors and not of the Foundation, its Trustees, or its staff. Publication by Russell Sage, therefore, does not imply Foundation endorsement.

Library of Congress Cataloging-in-Publication Data

Grubb, W. Norton.
    Learning to work: the case for reintegrating job training and education /
W. Norton Grubb.
      p. cm.
    Includes bibliographical references and index.
    ISBN 0-87154-367-2 (cloth: alk. paper)
    1. Occupational training—United States. 2. Employees—Training of—United
States. 3. Basic education—United States. 4. Vocational education—United
States. 5. Education—United States. I. Title.
HD5715.2.G78 1996
331.25'92'0973—dc20   96-11204
             CIP

Text design by Rozlyn Coleman.

RUSSELL SAGE FOUNDATION
112 East 64th Street, New York, New York 10021
10 9 8 7 6 5 4 3 2 1

Contents

List of Abbreviations

ABE   Adult basic education
AFDC   Aid to Families with Dependent Children
AUL   Atlanta Urban League
CBO   Community-based organization
CET   Center for Employment Training
CETA   Comprehensive Employment and Training Act
CLMS   Continuous Longitudinal Manpower Survey
CWEP   Community Work Experience Program
GAIN   Greater Avenues for Independence (California)
GAO   General Accounting Office
GED   General equivalency degree
JOBS   Job Opportunities and Basic Skills Training
JSA   Job search assistance
JTPA   Job Training Partnership Act
MDRC   Manpower Demonstration Research Corporation
MDTA   Manpower Development Training Act
MFSP   Minority Female Single Parent [Demonstration]
OIC   Opportunities Industrialization Center
PIC   Private Industry Council
PSE   Public service employment
RFP   Request for proposal
SDA   Service delivery area
SIPP   Survey of Income and Program Participation
STEP   Summer Training and Employment Program
STWOA   School-to-Work Opportunities Act
WIN   Work Incentive Program
WOW   Wider Opportunities for Women

Preface and Acknowledgments

THIS BOOK gives me another opportunity to pursue what I think of as an "integrationist" perspective. That is, the fragmentation of public programs in many different spheres has been detrimental, and a reintegration is necessary. I have previously explored at great length the integration of academic and vocational education (see, for example, Grubb, 1995a); as readers will see in chapter 7, I am quite taken with the vision underlying the School-to-Work Opportunities Act and its three forms of integration: academic and vocational education, secondary and postsecondary programs, and school-based and work-based learning. And, of greatest relevance to this book, I find it useful to think about the entire *system* of work-related education and job training—a system that is often fragmented and chaotic, to be sure, but one in which the components often act in coordinated ways to provide more effective services (Grubb and McDonnell, 1991, 1996; McDonnell and Grubb, 1991). I argue—particularly in chapters 6 and 7—that the education and job training components of this ragged system need to be better integrated, reversing the separation that first took place in the early 1960s. Such an integration is particularly important because the consolidation of federal education and training programs that will surely take place sometime in 1996 presents both challenges and opportunities to states to create their own coherent systems, and the approach I develop in chapter 7 is one way to do so.

An earlier version of this book, commissioned by the Training Policy and Programme Development Branch of the International Labour Office (ILO) in Geneva, has been published as *Evaluating Job Training Programs in the United States: Evidence and Explanations* (Grubb, 1995b). I thank

J. Gaude of the ILO for his support of that volume. I received helpful comments on an early draft of this manuscript from Tom Bailey, Fred Doolittle, Gregg Duncan, J. Gaude, Andrew Hahn, and Jim Riccio. I also thank the numerous individuals who were kind enough to provide documents, information, and perspectives on the job training programs, including Fred Doolittle, Judith Greissman, Jim Kemple, Ed Pauly, and Jim Riccio at the Manpower Demonstration Research Corporation; Larry Orr at Abt Associates; Martin Carnoy at Stanford University; Jan Watterworth at Mathematica Policy Research; and Paul Osterman at the Massachusetts Institute of Technology.

Finally, a good deal of my own research on the relationships among education and training programs, and on postsecondary occupational education, has been supported by the National Center for Research in Vocational Education (NCRVE) at the University of California, Berkeley, under grants from the U.S. Department of Education. The opinions expressed in this book are mine alone, and their publication does not necessarily constitute an endorsement by the ILO, the Department of Education, NCRVE, or any other entity.

W. Norton Grubb

Chapter 1

The Separation of Job Training from Education

S INCE THE 1960s, the institutions in the United States that educate and train people for employment have grown in number and complexity. High schools, the traditional locus of vocational education, still provide some job-specific education, but increasingly vocational education takes place in postsecondary institutions, including community colleges, technical institutes, and area vocational schools. The development of job training programs, first through manpower programs during the 1960s and then under the Comprehensive Employment and Training Act (CETA) during the 1970s and the Job Training Partnership Act (JTPA) during the 1980s, added to the number of programs, as have job training programs provided through the welfare system, especially the Job Opportunities and Basic Skills Training (JOBS) program of the Family Support Act of 1988. Other special-purpose programs have proliferated, including those for dislocated workers—individuals who become unemployed as a result of economic dislocations beyond their control, like the decline of defense industries or competition from foreign producers. Many states have initiated their own economic development programs, providing still other training resources intended to lure employment from other areas, facilitate local expansion, or forestall employers from leaving the area. Proprietary schools have also increased their enrollments, partly in response to increased student aid during the

1

1970s. Thus the "system" of work-related education and training institutions—those that consciously prepare individuals for relatively specific occupations that do not require a baccalaureate degree—has become increasingly complex and variegated.

In large part, the expansion of job training programs has reflected a concern with particular economic problems, especially those of unemployment, underemployment, and poverty. Job training programs were first discussed as a response to the unemployment created by the 1960–61 recession. Since then, periods of recession and unemployment, and specific kinds of unemployment (like the increases in the number of workers unemployed as a result of substantial economic changes), have generated interest in job training programs as potential solutions. And the expansion of welfare programs during the 1960s generated the realization that poverty was not likely to wither away of its own accord. One solution has been to propose job training. Because the problems of poverty, unemployment, and underemployment are closely related, it is not surprising that a number of job training programs have substantially similar methods, despite a proliferation of specific programs for specific purposes.

In large part, the federal government has elaborated the overall system of education and job training by establishing job training programs that are distinct from, and fiscally independent of, the education programs funded largely by states and localities in high schools, two- and four-year colleges, technical institutes, and area vocational schools. In the process, an important distinction has emerged between *education* and *job training*. The difference is not always clear, since some short-term, job-specific education programs look quite similar to job training; for example, some short-term programs in fields like clerical skills, computer applications, and electronics in both JTPA programs and area vocational schools last around fifteen weeks. However, there are at least seven differences between education and job training.

First, job training programs are generally much shorter than education programs. Many job training programs involve from ten to fifteen weeks of part-day attendance, so that the number of contact hours may be as low as forty; the average length of the programs studied in the recent JTPA evaluation was 3.5 months (Orr and others, 1994, exhibit 3.18). In contrast, the shortest common postsecondary education programs, those that lead to occupational certificates, generally last two semesters (about thirty weeks) of full-time enrollment, involving 360–1,000 contact hours; and two-year associate degree programs dominate community colleges. Of course, student attendance patterns can reduce these longer education programs to individual courses, and area vocational schools often offer short programs of part-time attendance over one semester of about fifteen weeks; therefore, some education programs are no more intensive than most job training programs.

Second, education programs, particularly in community colleges, other two-year colleges, and area vocational schools, are generally open to all members of the population, but job training programs are open only to those who are eligible—for example, the long-term unemployed or dislocated workers under JTPA or welfare recipients in welfare-to-work programs. (The issue of eligibility reflects the origin of job training as a solution to particular economic problems: only those who have suffered from these problems, not the population as a whole, are eligible.) By construction, then, job training programs enroll individuals who have had particular problems in employment; while some problems may be due to overall employment conditions, others may be due to deficient skills, behavioral problems, and other personal traits.

Third, most education programs take place in educational institutions that are well institutionalized and standardized—high schools, community colleges, and four-year colleges. In contrast, job training services are offered in a bewildering variety of educational institutions, community-based organizations (CBOs), firms, unions, and proprietary schools, making it difficult to determine how services are organized and provided.[1]

Fourth, the kinds of services provided in education programs are relatively standard. For the most part they offer classroom instruction via both academic and vocational courses, often including labs, workshops, and other hands-on activities. Job training programs offer classroom instruction, too, both in basic (or remedial) academic subjects like reading, writing, and math and in vocational skills, but they also offer on-the-job training, which places individuals in work sites to learn on the job;[2] work experience, in which individuals work for short periods of time; job search assistance, in which clients receive training in how to look for work, write résumés, file job applications, interview for jobs, and the like; and job clubs, which require clients to spend a certain amount of time looking for jobs. Some programs provide counseling as well on labor market opportunities and "life skills" like the ability to plan. Job training programs also support placement efforts somewhat more often than educational institutions do, reflecting another division between education and job training: those in educational institutions are likely to declare that they are responsible for "education, not employment," while those in job training are more likely to accept that they have a responsibility for placing individuals as well as training them appropriately. Unfortunately, the variety of such services is so great and the forms they take are so varied that it is often difficult to know precisely what takes place in a job training program. As a result, the evaluations of specific program components (reviewed in chap. 5) are often not particularly comprehensive, and conclusions about the effectiveness of particular services are hard to draw.

Fifth, the goals of education programs are typically quite broad, encompassing political, moral, and intellectual purposes as well as occupational ends, but job training programs focus exclusively on preparing individuals to become employed. In the case of welfare-to-work programs, the single goal is to get welfare recipients employed as quickly as possible so they can move off the welfare rolls. Because the goal of job training programs is so unambiguous and because job training yields no intrinsic benefits (no one would declare that being in a job training program is fun, a social activity, or a normal part of growing up, as Americans might say about schools and colleges), there has been a long history of evaluating programs to ascertain their effectiveness. These evaluations have become increasingly sophisticated over time; certainly they are much more sophisticated than those of education programs. The results have influenced public policy in a way that evaluations of the education system have not because the political pressures in education—the support of parents for programs that benefit their own children, including such diverse offerings as those aimed at low-income, limited-English-speaking, or gifted students, for example—are generally lacking in job training programs, for which the only justification for public support is the reductions they bring about in unemployment, poverty, and the receipt of welfare.

Sixth, job training has generally been a federal initiative, and many job training programs are wholly federally funded though locally administered. The important exceptions are welfare-related programs like those in JOBS, which are partly state funded because welfare (Aid to Families with Dependent Children) has always been funded through grants requiring states to match federal revenues in order to receive federal funds. In contrast, most education, including postsecondary occupational education, is a state and local responsibility, with federal funding constituting only a small fraction of overall support. (The only exceptions are private proprietary schools that receive substantial federal support through student aid, but the roughly comparable public institutions—community colleges and technical institutes—do not.) One consequence of the difference in funding sources is that job training programs have been administratively distinct from education programs because federal funds flow to different agencies, and states often view job training programs as federal programs rather than as "theirs." While a few states have been relatively active in creating coherent job training policies, most have been relatively inactive in programs that lack any state funding, like those falling under JTPA (McDonnell and Zellman, 1993). In addition, job training has always been much more vulnerable to federal legislative changes, including the cuts in fiscal support that are likely in the mid- to late 1990s.

Finally, job training programs differ from education programs in that they constitute a separate system, a "second-chance" system in some ways parallel to but disconnected from the "first-chance" educational system. Over the course of one hundred fifty years, the education system in the United States has developed a well-articulated series of offerings from kindergarten (now often extended to preschool programs) to the university level. But for those who have left this system without adequate skills, the job training system can be a second chance to enter the mainstream of the labor force. In general, the establishment of this second-chance system is one manifestation of a generous American impulse: to provide opportunities to individuals through various forms of learning and to include all who might benefit from such activities. However, this second-chance system is much younger than the education system; it spends less, is more disorganized, has a lower status, and is poorly institutionalized so that it cannot resist purely political pressures. As a result, it has been subject to revision by nearly every president, so that it lacks the stability of the education system.

In this volume I review the effectiveness of job training programs in the United States, concentrating on the most recent and most sophisticated evaluations.[3] My purpose is not principally to review the *methodology* of these evaluations (though I review some important methodological issues in chap. 3); such reviews, often highly technical and inconclusive, are unlikely to change the political consensus around job training or to suggest ways of reforming the current system. Instead, I emphasize the *outcomes* of these programs, which have been roughly consistent despite great variation in the kinds of programs offered and in evaluation methods.

Chapter 2 describes the types of job training programs that I examine, explaining why it is appropriate to consider a wide variety of programs. Chapter 3 outlines the preferred methodology in recent evaluations, random assignment, and clarifies both the strengths of this approach and its inevitable weaknesses. In chapter 4 I present a series of results, first for job training programs, then for welfare-to-work programs, and finally for special experimental programs. Following in chapter 5 is a discussion of the outcomes of job training programs in regard to different population groups, different types of service, the effects of programs over time, and different programs. Finally, in the last section of chapter 5, I present some recent cost-benefit analyses to examine whether job training programs are "worth doing" in the sense that their benefits outweigh their costs. A series of tables drawn from the evaluations accompanies these two chapters so that the reader can see the results of the major evaluations and assess the effects of job training programs independently of my analysis.

The major question these evaluations address is whether job training programs have been successes or failures, particularly as measured by employment, annual earnings, and reductions in welfare payments. A conventional reading of the evaluations is that many (though not all) job training programs lead to small but statistically significant increases in employment and earnings and (for welfare recipients) small decreases in welfare payments. The cost-benefit analyses that have been done show that the social benefits usually (but not always) outweigh the costs, so most of these programs are worth doing in a cost-benefit sense. One might conclude that job training has been successful and should be continued. However, the gains in employment and earnings are quite small from a practical standpoint: they are insufficient to move individuals out of poverty or off welfare; their effects very often decay over time, so that even the small benefits are short lived; and, as they are currently constructed, they certainly do not give individuals a chance at middle-class occupations or incomes.[4] In my interpretation, therefore, the successes of job training programs have been quite modest, even trivial—and that dismal conclusion begs for some explanation. In chapter 6, therefore, I present a series of possible explanations for the weak results of job training programs. The reasons for failure are necessarily more speculative than are the outcome results in chapters 4 and 5, which are based on harder data and (in many cases) sophisticated evaluation methods, but some understanding of why job training programs have had such modest results is necessary to develop recommendations on how to remedy such programs through public policy or to create more effective programs from the start.

In particular, many of the problems I identify originate in the separation of job training from education. As I argue in chapter 6, this separation has certainly worked to the detriment of job training by creating programs that are too short, too focused on immediate employment rather than on the enhancement of skills, unaware of pedagogical issues, and independent of related efforts. But the separation has also undermined education programs by segregating from them the kinds of services—outreach, placement, work-based instruction—that would benefit many students, and the focus on outcomes that is more typical of job training programs is usually lacking in educational efforts. This observation provides one rationale for reintegrating education and job training.

Although the benefits of current job training programs have been small, the problems they address—unemployment, underemployment, and welfare dependency—are too serious to ignore. Therefore, the appropriate response is to reform job training programs rather than abandon them. In chapter 7 I therefore present a vision of how job training programs could be structured to avoid the reasons for failure outlined in chapter 6. This vision has been embodied in current federal legislation (the School-to-Work Opportunities Act, passed in May 1994) that applies to high schools and community colleges. Its implications for job training programs have not yet developed, so my purpose in chapter 7 is to clarify how reforms proposed for the education system might benefit job training programs as well. I therefore present a vision of how to knit existing vocational education and job training programs into an overall system that creates vertical "ladders" of ever-expanding opportunities. In the end such reforms could eliminate the unproductive division between education and job training that has developed since the 1960s.

The potential direction of the education and job training system is particularly important because of current debates in Washington. In many areas of federal policy Congress is now debating proposals for consolidating federal programs by combining the myriad federal programs (see table 2.1 for education and training programs) into a small number of block grants for states to use with greater freedom. At this writing the details of consolidation—which programs would be included, what federal restrictions would continue to be imposed, what the state governance mechanism would be—remain murky, and it is pointless to speculate about the specific form consolidation will take. In general, consolidation is a response to the sense that too many overlapping programs have the potential for too much waste and duplication, though it also represents an effort simply to reduce the amount of federal funding. Of course, consolidation does not solve the problems associated with too many programs working at cross-purposes; it merely throws the issue to the states to resolve in fifty different ways. But consolidation presents states with opportunity as well as danger, and the vision in chapter 7 is one that states could use as a response both to the ineffectiveness of current job training programs and to the challenge of creating coherent systems of education and job training.

Chapter 2

The Nature of Job Training Programs

S EVERAL different strands of development have created the current "system" of training programs—in reality, a nonsystem with a bewildering variety of purposes, services, and funding. One strand began with manpower programs established in 1962 in response to the recession of 1960–61. The Manpower Development Training Act (MDTA) of 1962 established training programs administered by the Department of Labor and separate from federal support of vocational education.[1] An independent funding mechanism for programs outside the schools was established in part because of the poor reputation of vocational education and in part because of a general feeling that secondary schools were not equipped to provide nontraditional training for adults. These programs were then consolidated in the Comprehensive Employment and Training Act of 1973. Like the programs it combined, CETA provided little role for state governments and gave local administrative units greater decision-making power over the types of training offered, the groups of individuals served, and the institutions offering training and other services.

States were given additional authority by the Job Training Partnership Act, the successor to CETA, enacted in 1983. State governments now designate local service delivery areas (SDAs), and they can establish priorities for an SDA's use of a portion of the federal grant. However, JTPA still remains a federal rather than a state program, as nearly all funding comes from the federal government and federal regulations apply to all programs nationwide. A few states have been relatively active: most have established priorities for coordinating job training with vocational education, some have used JTPA as part of an overall welfare-to-work policy, and some have used it as an economic development tool to try to lure employment from other states. A very few states—for example, Maine, Maryland, Minnesota, New Jersey, and West Virginia—have included JTPA programs in efforts to integrate their entire employment and training systems. But such activist policies have been comparatively rare; many states have served merely as funding conduits and administrators of federal policy rather than make any effort to assert a state role beyond that required by federal regulation (McDonnell and Zellman, 1993).

The development of job training programs did more than simply add new funding sources for work-related training; it also dramatically changed the types of institutions that provide training. Job training programs since the 1960s have been characterized by their use of community-based organizations, unions, private firms, proprietary schools, and other institutions—private alternatives to conventional high schools, community colleges, and technical colleges—to provide training and related services. This aspect of job training has given the education and training system greater variety and fluidity and has helped erode the boundary between public and private programs.

Job training also marked a turn toward private sector participation in public programs, not only with the funding of private organizations such as CBOs but also with the establishment by JTPA of Private Industry Councils (PICs), at least 51 percent of whose members must represent the private sector. The PICs are responsible for policy guidance and program oversight, and they must approve SDA training plans. They also have the option to administer JTPA programs directly, although fewer than 20 percent do so. It is important to note that private sector representation refers to employers, not representatives of labor, such as unions. Overall, the participation of unions in the job training system is relatively weak, partly because they now represent only 11 percent of the employees in the United States.

JTPA also differs from earlier programs in the nature of the mandates it imposes. While its predecessors focused on the types of services that local agencies could deliver, JTPA emphasizes outcomes by requiring that SDAs meet specific performance standards. For most of its history, the federal government identified twelve standards from which states selected eight that SDAs must meet;[2] states could add standards of their own and could use either a federal adjustment model or one of their own design to take into account the demographic and labor market characteristics of individual SDAs. In theory, the imposition of performance standards is a way of making JTPA more effective. In practice, however, performance standards have proved to be uncorrelated with the effects measured by more sophisticated evaluation techniques (Doolittle and others, 1993, p. 10). The reason is that sophisticated evaluations of the kind summarized in chapters 4 and 5 compare the effects of programs with what similar individuals accomplish in the absence of programs; in contrast, performance measures examine only the behavior of program participants without comparing them with any other group and have been susceptible to manipulation by local programs. In general, performance measures have made local programs concerned with the details of performance measures but not necessarily with effectiveness in a broader sense.

A second strand of development has concentrated on welfare recipients. Historically, welfare in the United States—principally the program known as Aid to Families with Dependent Children (AFDC)—was provided only to mothers with children so they could stay at home and care for them.[3] However, as working has become more common for all women in the United States, including mothers of young children, pressure has increased to get welfare mothers (and fathers) into employment and off the welfare rolls.[4] The first efforts were established in 1962 in the Community Work and Training Program. Like MDTA, it bypassed the vocational education system by providing funds from the Department of Labor for welfare programs at the local level to use. The Economic Opportunity Act of 1964 included yet another program designed to encourage work, the Work Experience and Training Program. In 1967, as part of the far-reaching Amendments to the Social Security Act, the Work Incentive (WIN) program was established as a voluntary work program. Although WIN was made mandatory for welfare recipients in 1971, it was not funded at a level that made widespread participation enforceable and therefore remained a limited and voluntary program.

Another strand of President Lyndon Johnson's War on Poverty was the "services strategy" developed as an antidote to poverty. This strategy provided a variety of support services (such as child care and transportation) to enable welfare recipients to work their way off welfare. As embodied in the 1967 Amendments to the Social Security Act, it included funding for short-term training. The support services, which were consolidated in the Title XX Amendments of 1973, allocated funds to states for social services and gave states greater authority to decide which services to provide. Title XX emerged largely intact (though with considerably reduced funding) in the Social Services Block Grant, enacted in 1981. However, in practice, work-related services (including training) were rarely provided under Title XX, which focused on rehabilitating families on welfare and preventing abuse rather than on facilitating employment (Dickinson, 1986).

In 1981, the Reagan administration, building on a history of welfare-to-work programs that forced welfare recipients to work in exchange for grants, allowed states to develop their own programs for getting welfare recipients back to work. Not surprisingly, the state programs that developed were enormously varied. Most relied heavily on job search (short-term assistance in applying for work but no other training or support services) and work experience or on-the-job training, both accomplished through short-term job placements. A few developed Community Work Experience Programs (CWEPs), in which welfare recipients provide community service in amounts related to the size of their grants. Such programs are equivalent to the traditional conception of workfare, in which individuals work in exchange for welfare grants. Although 84 percent of the programs offered vocational skills training and 72 percent provided post–high school education, in practice only 2.3 percent of the welfare recipients participating in these programs received any skill training, and only 1.6 percent enrolled in postsecondary education (mostly in Massachusetts, Michigan, and California). In fact, only 3.2 percent received remedial education; even the most basic forms of education and training were quite rare.[5] In practice, then, experimentation with various kinds of services and welfare-to-work strategies led to an emphasis on job search rather than on education, training, or other services.[6]

The most recent development in this area was the Family Support Act of 1988, which required all states to establish Job Opportunities and Basic Skills Training programs to increase the employment of welfare recipients. The legislation provided federal matching funds ranging from 50 percent to 72 percent of total costs for a variety of work-related services—including job search, work experience, counseling, child care, and other support services—and all forms of remedial education, vocational education, and training. States had considerable flexibility in determining what services to provide, who would provide them, and what the scope of programs would be.[7] Although most states have increased their total spending for welfare-related job training, the level varies greatly, perpetuating the differences in welfare benefits and services among states. Many state legislatures have never appropriated sufficient funds to match the maximum federal funding, so that the potential of JOBS to provide additional training for welfare recipients has never been fully realized.

In JOBS, Congress crafted a program that combined the services strategy of the 1960s with the work-related emphasis of WIN, including the use of education and training. It contained a mandate, since participation is mandatory for all AFDC recipients who are single heads of households and who have no children under three years of age;[8] inducements in the form of services (for example, one year of health care after participants obtain a job, and transitional child care) to reduce the cost of moving from welfare to employment; and capacity building through longer-term investments in education and training (typically up to two years). As it has done with vocational education and JTPA programs, the federal government has attempted to target JOBS to those recipients most in need. To avoid a situation in which states primarily serve those most likely to leave the welfare system even without additional assistance, the federal government requires states to spend 55 percent of their JOBS funds on those most at risk of long-term welfare dependency (for example, young mothers who are high school dropouts).

To some extent, the federal government has specified the services states can provide by designating which ones are reimbursable. It has also defined service levels fairly specifically. For example, the proposed JOBS regulations specified that states could count as JOBS participants only those people who were spending at least twenty hours a week in authorized activities. The states protested vigorously, arguing that some effective education and training programs require fewer than twenty hours a week (a full community college course load typically includes twelve to fifteen hours of classroom contact per week). The U.S. Department of Health and Human Services subsequently changed the regulations to make the twenty-hour requirement the average for groups of participants (Kosterlitz, 1989).

Still other job training programs have been developed in response to other problems. For example, a number of programs provide assistance specifically for veterans, since disabled veterans often have a difficult time entering the labor force; dislocated worker programs have expanded because of the need to retrain experienced workers laid off through no fault of their own (for example, because of the decline of the timber industry in some states, the decline of the defense and aerospace industries in other states, or the possibility of unemployment because of the North American Free Trade Agreement, particularly in border states) for other kinds of employment; and vocational rehabilitation programs have focused on the special employment problems of disabled individuals. Congress has often responded to new problems with new programs rather than incorporate new purposes into old programs; this tendency in turn has generated a proliferation of job training programs with roughly the same goal—the enhancement of employment—for different groups with varying barriers to employment.

A particular concern has been the development of programs for youths. The problem of high school dropouts is an old one, dating almost to the turn of the century, but it has become increasingly serious as the employment prospects of dropouts have become worse relative to those for high school graduates. In addition, programs for youths have the special aura of prevention: if they can steer individuals away from unemployment and away from crime, drugs, and (for girls) early pregnancy, then they can prevent costly social problems in the future. In response, a large number of programs, particularly within CETA and then under JTPA, have focused on the employment of youths, both those who have dropped out of high school and those still in school but considered likely to drop out— and their effectiveness is a subject of special concern. Some of these programs are properly considered job training programs—that is, they offer education and training to equip young people with new skills—while others are really work experience programs, particularly summer youth programs. A positive view is that work experience itself will teach young people the personal attributes necessary for stable employment; a more general perspective is that such efforts are palliatives to keep troublesome youths off the streets. I consider the effects of programs targeted for youths under JTPA and in experimental programs, and of programs for other populations, in chapters 4 and 5 and interpret the especially dismal results for youths in chapter 6.

The result of these many strands of development is that a bewildering array of job training programs exists. Indeed, a U.S. General Accounting Office (GAO) examination of federally funded employment and training programs counted 163 programs spending $20.4 billion in 1995 (U.S. General Accounting Office, 1995b).[9] These figures are somewhat misleading, since they disaggregate different titles of certain programs (for example, JTPA is counted as twenty programs because of its different

Table 2.1 Federal Appropriations for Employment and Job Training Programs, Fiscal Year 1995 (Millions of Dollars)

Agency and Program	Appropriation
Department of Labor	
Job Training Partnership Act	4,912.5
Veterans programs	175.1
Employment service	845.9
Other	910.5
Department of Education	
Vocational education	1,236.2
Adult education	270.6
Literacy programs	38.5
Student grants and loans	4,716.0
Rehabilitation services	2,086.1
Other	638.0
Department of Health and Human Services	
Job Opportunities and Basic Skills Training	1,300.0
Community Services Block Grants	426.3
Refugee assistance	105.0
Other	192.3
Department of Agriculture	
Food stamp employment and training	165.0
Department of Housing and Urban Development	
Youthbuild	50.0
Empowerment Zone and Enterprise Community Program	640.0
Other	47.3
Other departments	1,763.3
Total	20,413.9

Source: U.S. General Accounting Office (1995), appendix II.

sections), they include education programs (like literacy efforts and student grants and loans) that are only distantly related to job preparation, and they include other programs (like Community Development Block Grants) that fund a variety of services in addition to job training. Still, the count illustrates nicely the proliferation of programs, each in response to slightly different problems, and it reflects the widespread perception of how incoherent and fragmented the education and training "system" has become. Table 2.1 summarizes the GAO figures on federal education and job training programs and shows the rough magnitudes of different programs. Clearly the major programs are JTPA and JOBS, which are larger than any other federal program with the exception of student grants and loans for postsecondary education and rehabilitation services for the disabled.[10]

Finally, a large number of experimental programs, often started by private foundations, have tested particular approaches to enhancing employment. Some of these efforts have been particularly intensive, and others have concentrated on providing services of particularly high quality. They therefore might yield information about what excellent job training programs—well designed, independent of political manipulation, and freed of having to operate under normal pressures—could accomplish. Several of these experimental programs have been carefully evaluated, and I present the results of those evaluations in chapter 4 with the caveat that such programs may be quite different from those operated with public funding.[11]

There are several reasons for examining the evaluations of a variety of job training programs rather than confining a review to the main job programs of JTPA. One is that job programs overlap considerably because of the ways they have been established. JOBS programs for welfare recipients often send their clients to local JTPA programs, sometimes on their own initiative and sometimes at the state's directive, so the two programs use the same services and providers. Both JTPA and JOBS programs may send their clients to vocational education in community colleges, area vocational schools, and technical institutes, particularly when clients are able to find their own education and training arrangements (known as individual referral) or when there is a fiscal incentive to do so.[12] Second, the services various job training programs provide overlap considerably, so that information from one program is useful in judging the effectiveness of others. Finally, the discussions of job training programs in the United States generally commingle information about different types of programs, so it is necessary to understand the evaluations of all these programs.

Chapter 3

The Methodology of Job Training Evaluations

THE FIRST round of job training programs, those begun in the 1960s under the Manpower Development Training Act, were evaluated with less sophisticated methods than are now standard. (See table 4.1 and the associated discussion.) Effectiveness was very much an issue when job training programs were consolidated in the Comprehensive Employment and Training Act in 1973 because of suspicions that many of the manpower training programs of the 1960s were not especially effective. The CETA program therefore generated a huge number of evaluation documents that take up literally several yards of shelf space (summarized in Taggart, 1981). The quantitative evaluations of CETA used quasi-experimental regression methods to compare CETA enrollees and comparison groups with similar characteristics (gender, race, education, labor market experience, and the like).[1] In addition, a number of studies administered surveys to CETA trainees about their experiences, others described the nature of training in great detail, and still others, using what might be called ethnographic techniques, observed individual programs closely to see what was going on. These studies generated information on employment outcomes, but they also described many other dimensions of programs.

Beginning in the 1980s, pressured by the limitations of quasi-experimental methods, outcome evaluators began to use true experimental

17

methods for evaluation:[2] the researchers recruited individuals for programs and allowed a random sample (the "experimentals") to enroll in the program. By administering questionnaires to those who did not enroll (the "controls"), they collected roughly the same information from the controls and the experimentals about the services they received and their employment histories. The studies avoided the ethical dilemmas involved in experimental methods by using volunteer subjects and by recruiting more individuals than the program under evaluation could accommodate, so that one could argue that some individuals would not be served even if the programs were not being evaluated using an experimental design. In addition, the effectiveness of these programs was genuinely unknown, so that, unlike denying an individual access to a vaccine known to work against a particular disease, the experimental method kept no individuals out of a program that would surely increase their life chances.

The great advantage of experimental methods is that they can eliminate the possibility that various factors unconnected to program effectiveness are responsible for any findings. In job training programs, three such factors are particularly dangerous: selection effects, maturation effects, and regression to the mean. *Selection effects* operate because job training programs by construction select those individuals who have certain barriers to employment—low education levels, little work history, perhaps motivational problems or histories of drug and alcohol abuse—and therefore might be expected to benefit least from any training program; the variety of these characteristics is so great and so unmeasurable that it is difficult to create an equivalent control group without experimental methods.

These *negative* selection effects are complicated by other selection effects created by the administration of programs and by economic conditions. To look good, job training programs have an incentive to choose the most able and job ready of the individuals who are eligible—a process known as *creaming*. Creaming creates a *positive* selection effect in addition to the negative selection effect involved in eligibility for the program. Moreover, the positive selection effect may operate differently over the business cycle: when unemployment falls, the most job-ready individuals are able to find jobs, so programs have to work harder to recruit people to enroll—and may have to enroll the least job-ready individuals with multiple employment problems. Paradoxically, in boom times, when low unemployment makes placements somewhat easier, the individuals enrolled are the least job ready; when unemployment is high and placements are more difficult, the most job-ready individuals are likely to be enrolled because of creaming. It is thus virtually impossible to construct a control group that is comparable to the individuals enrolled in job training programs except under experimental conditions, since too many administrative, economic, and personal factors affect the composition of a job training program.

In addition, *maturation effects* occur when individuals improve their conditions by aging or maturing. These effects are particularly likely for youths, who suffer much higher rates of unemployment and lower earnings when they are young and gradually mature into the relatively stable employment and earnings patterns of adults, most without the help of any particular program (Klerman and Karoly, 1994). Maturation effects are also likely in measures of academic achievement, knowledge about the labor market, risk-taking behavior, and certain measures of disruptive behavior, including drug use and criminal activity. Without considering this phenomenon, youth programs may look effective over time as those who have enrolled in them mature, even though the program may have had no effect on this process.

Regression to the mean is another problem in evaluating programs. By construction, job training programs enroll individuals who have had problems in employment. But some of these individuals may have had an unlucky spell—for example, individuals with adequate job skills who are laid off unexpectedly in an otherwise healthy local economy or dislocated workers whose layoffs are due to a firm's closing—and they can be expected to find employment on their own within a few months. That is, they regress back to their normal conditions of employment after a short period. For such individuals a job training program might speed up the return to employment but not make any difference in whether they find employment again, unlike individuals who lack fundamental job skills and are unlikely to find employment without training. Regression to the mean is particularly prevalent in welfare programs: a large fraction of the welfare population is on welfare for a brief period following a layoff, the departure of a wage-earning family member like a husband, or a medical emergency, but many find employment and leaves the welfare rolls after a short period of time. If large numbers of these "temporary" welfare recipients are enrolled in job training programs, then the programs will appear to be successful even though normal turnover rather than the effectiveness of the program may cause the apparent increase in employment. In the quasi-experimental evaluations of CETA programs in the late 1970s, the apparently greater increase in earnings for experimental groups than for comparison groups turned out to be due to regression to the mean for males, though for females job training programs increased earnings by slightly more than would be expected from such a pattern (Bloom and McLaughlin, 1982; see figure 4.1).

However, experimental methods eliminate every kind of selection effect as well as maturation effects and regression to the mean, so that any differences in employment after a job training program can be attributed to the program rather than to other causes.[3] As a result of these methods, job training programs have been more carefully evaluated than any other kind of social program, and the results summarized in chapters 4 and 5 surely reflect the effects of the programs themselves, not the limits of imperfect research methods. Despite their power, however, the use of experimental methods in evaluation still involves a number of disadvantages and problems.[4]

Experimental methods sometimes treat the program as a black box (a treatment whose nature is unknown). Learning that a program increases earnings may not be especially valuable in determining which elements of a successful program are effective and need to be incorporated in any replications. While more recent evaluations have become somewhat better at analyzing the effects of particular services, studies still tend to treat evaluation as a *statistical* problem—ascertaining whether a variable Y (say, earnings) is caused by a variable X (say, program participation)—rather than by a *programmatic* problem—determining what kinds of services offered to which individuals reduce unemployment, poverty, and welfare payments.

The nonrandom behavior of experimental groups can affect even the best-designed experiments and in the process weaken some of the advantages of experimental methods. For example, the most recent evaluations of Job Training Partnership Act programs chose experimental groups to enroll in job training, but only a fraction actually did so since some of those assigned to job training (the "assignees") lost their motivation, moved away, or for some other reason did not enroll. Those who failed to enroll are likely to be the least motivated, the least organized, and the most plagued by problems that affect employment. As a result, the average increase in earnings among assignees was lower than it was among those who enrolled in the programs—and evaluators disagree on whether to use the benefit per *assignee* or per *enrollee* in deciding whether the program works.[5] Similarly, attrition in the course of job training programs is nonrandom since those who complete programs are likely to be more able and motivated. And in the evaluation of Florida's Project Independence, some members of the control group, which was supposed to have no access to special services, by mistake were allowed to attend an orientation session and to participate in some Project Independence activities, "contaminating" the difference between the treatment group and the control group (Kemple, Friedlander, and Fellerath, 1995). Thus even well-designed experiments can turn into quasi experiments, with some of the most interesting results affected by nonrandom effects.

An evaluation that assigns volunteers randomly to a job training program or to a control group may not use random assignment for other issues of interest. For example, job training typically uses a mix of classroom instruction in vocational skills, basic academic skills instruction (or remediation), on-the-job training or work experience, and job search assistance. But even though volunteers may be assigned randomly to a *program,* they are typically not assigned randomly to the *services* within that program. If programs match individuals to services, then (for example) they may assign the least job-ready individuals to longer-term basic skills instruction but give the most job-ready individuals job search assistance. This matching process might make job search assistance look effective while making basic instruction look ineffective. Under these conditions the effects of being in a program are evaluated experimentally, but the effects of different services can be evaluated only with quasi-experimental methods, so some evaluations have failed to conclude anything about the effects of different services. In addition, sample sizes affect any conclusions: if the numbers receiving any particular service are small, then conclusions about effectiveness are difficult to make within the normal limits of statistical significance.

The problems affecting the evaluation of different services also influence the evaluation of program effectiveness for different subgroups within the population—for example, women compared with men, high school graduates compared with dropouts, or those with more labor market experience compared to those with little experience. Job training programs may be effective for certain subgroups but not for others. One important question is whether job training is most effective for the least job-ready (in which case creaming should definitely be avoided) or the most job-ready individuals.

In many evaluations, individuals in the control group are able to get education and training on their own, so the program evaluated may not greatly increase the services provided to them. Recent evaluations have documented this process much more carefully than some of the early ones did, so that the real differences in services received are apparent, but the process still creates a problem for evaluators: if both experimental and control groups receive roughly the same services, then there will be no difference in outcomes and the effectiveness of the program cannot be measured.

The problems in evaluating the effectiveness of different services for different subgroups extend to the evaluation of particular programs. That is, a national job training program like JTPA is in reality an agglomeration of over five hundred programs, each administered locally. Any *average* effect masks the *distribution* around this average caused by the existence of highly effective programs simultaneously with truly dreadful local ones. Because the most effective programs may be the most valuable guides to improving practice, if they can be identified their characteristics may provide the best information about how to improve programs. While the early evaluations did not address the effectiveness of individual programs, some of the most recent evaluations have managed to detect programs that are more effective than the average (see the review in chap. 5).

Evaluations that focus on individuals in job training programs can determine whether the likelihood of employment is greater for the enrolled group than for a control group, but they cannot tell whether the aggregate employment in a region increases. It is possible that the employment of participants in job training programs comes at the expense of others who would have received those jobs had there been no job training program; that is, a job training program merely displaces some potential workers with others.[6] This is particularly likely to be the case if a "training" program establishes strong relationships with employers, in effect becoming a preferred source of moderately skilled labor by serving as a screening mechanism for motivation, stability, or other traits that particular employers want without providing much training. One could argue that such displacement effects will be captured by the control group, which by construction includes those who might otherwise have gotten the jobs that trainees receive, but the small size of control groups relative to the pool of potential workers makes this argument seem unlikely. To my knowledge no study has examined the potential extent of such displacement effects.

The danger of displacement also reflects a difference between human capital models of earnings and employment, in which education and training provide new competencies that increase the productivity and then the wages and earnings of individuals, and screening and signaling models, in which education or job training signals the greater competencies of certain individuals over others but does not change those competencies.

If screening prevails, then individuals completing job training programs will have higher levels of employment and earnings than those not completing such programs, but their employment will come at the expense of other individuals who fail to get these jobs and employment and productivity in the aggregate will not increase. Job training programs often assume a human capital model, in which programs enhance their clients' competencies, ranging from cognitive abilities, to manipulative skills, to purely behavioral abilities such as motivation and persistence in employment. There is virtually no reference in the evaluation literature to the possibility that signaling might explain positive outcomes, although some administrators acknowledge that a few employers use them as screening mechanisms to distinguish motivated from unmotivated workers.

Because experimental evaluations are expensive and cannot rely on normal census methods of data collection, programs have typically been evaluated for only a relatively short period of time after participants complete them. For example, the period was thirty months in recent JTPA evaluations (Bloom and others, 1994), three years in the evaluation of the Greater Avenues for Independence program (Riccio, Friedlander, and Freedman, 1994), and four years in the evaluation of the experimental JOBSTART program (Cave and others, 1993). The longest job training evaluation collected information from several welfare-to-work programs five and six years after the completion of the program (Friedlander and Burtless, 1995). These evaluations are therefore quite different from the usual analyses of earnings patterns by levels of education, which typically analyze individuals between the ages of eighteen and sixty-five and can generate age-earnings profiles describing the effects of education at different ages.

The period of time for which a program is evaluated is critical because of the question of whether any potential benefits increase or degrade over time. In the pattern typical of age-earnings profiles for different education levels, for example, a level of schooling may not generate any real increase in earnings for several years, during which an individual is searching for an appropriate job; then the benefits tend to increase, peaking somewhere during the period between ages forty-five and fifty-five before declining as retirement begins. Similarly, in job training programs one might expect a *decrease* in earnings during the program itself as individuals are forced to leave any employment they have. Then, perhaps following a period of job search when earnings are still low, the hope is that earnings would be higher than those of the control group and would continue increasing as the skills from the job training program enable individuals to advance in their jobs. However, a different possibility is that short-term job training programs push individuals into low-quality employment without improving their skills so that they enjoy employment benefits that disappear after a period of time. The experimentals are no better off than the controls in the long run and are potentially even worse off because of the period of low earnings during the program itself. (This scenario may be especially dangerous in job search assistance, which is designed to help individuals find jobs without improving their skills.) The difference between these two possible patterns can be detected only with information about earnings several years after a program ends, and unfortunately many evaluations have not lasted long enough to collect such information. The available long-term results are reviewed in chapter 5.

Most evaluations have included outcomes of the greatest political interest: employment, earnings, the amounts of welfare payments received, and the question of whether individuals remain on welfare. In some cases evaluations have measured noneconomic outcomes, including the receipt of educational credentials, such as the general equivalency diploma; reproductive behavior, such as the number of children born; sexual behavior; criminal behavior; and drug use. (See, for example, tables 4.6, 4.13, and 5.6 on arrest rates, the effects of New Chance, and the benefits of Job Corps, respectively.) Some of the noneconomic measures are related to long-term prospects as well as being of interest for their own sake. While evaluations have tended to expand the kinds of outcomes considered, one serious omission remains: no study has examined the effects on the children of those enrolled in programs. This omission is important because the purpose of welfare (or Aid to Families with Dependent Children) has always been to protect children. But this goal often gets lost in policy debates, in which hostility toward low-income *parents* undermines the original purpose of supporting *children.* The tendency of evaluations to overlook children is partly a practical question and partly a reflection of political reality, but it also means that no information is available to counter the neglect of children in policy debates.

The predominance of experimental approaches has overshadowed other methods of understanding job training programs, particularly the use of qualitative and ethnographic evaluations that might provide better insights into why programs succeed or fail. The early evaluation literature on CETA and the welfare experiments of the 1970s included some qualitative studies, in which researchers observed programs carefully, interviewed participants at length, and otherwise tried to determine what life in a program was like for its participants. The purpose was not only to get a better sense of what programs were like—the "texture of daily life" or the "lived experience" of programs, as ethnographers might say—but also to develop better information about how programs are implemented, what precisely goes on in them, and why they might be ineffective.

In recent qualitative ethnographies and case studies, for example, Hull (1993) has described the amount of teaching about on-the-job relationships (in addition to technical skills) that occurs in a banking program; Kalman and Losey (1996) have analyzed how a workplace literacy program fails to live up to its self-conception as an innovative, worker-centered program; Gowen (1993) has described the turmoil in a workplace literacy program; Grubb and Kalman (1994) have described how the dominant teaching methods in work-related remedial programs undermine their effectiveness; and investigations based on interviews have suggested that certain behavioral problems make keeping (rather than finding) a job a problem among the chronically unemployed (Quint, Musick, and Ladner, 1994). This last study is particularly interesting because it examined the lives of fifty women enrolled in New Chance, which was also evaluated with random-assignment methods (see chap. 4 and table 4.13). The study found that those enrolled in the program were enthusiastic about it but that their progress into employment was slow and uneven partly because of the problems caused by living in highly disorganized families and communities.

One rationale for qualitative studies, then, is that they can provide explanations for the outcomes determined by quantitative analyses and indicate what improvements to programs might be necessary. Many of the reasons I offer in chapter 6 for the small benefits of job training programs are based not on formal results from random-assignment experiments but on informal case studies and observations. Formal quantitative evaluations are necessary because only they can demonstrate the effects of job training programs on employment and earnings, but qualitative studies are necessary to show why some programs work and others do not and to clarify how existing programs might be improved. Unfortunately, these two traditions of research are not well integrated: qualitative examinations typically collect no information about effects on earnings and employment, and quantitative analyses rarely carry out qualitative studies.

The final drawback of random-assignment evaluation is that it is expensive. It can therefore be applied to large-scale evaluations of national programs of considerable policy importance, but it cannot be applied routinely, to small programs, to many experimental efforts, or to local programs that are deciding what mix of services or which specific providers they should use. Job training programs thus have typically been subjected to two quite different kinds of "evaluation": random-assignment evaluations of great sophistication and cost, performed largely for federal policy makers deciding how to establish guidelines and legislation, and locally collected information about effectiveness, like the performance measures required by JTPA and information about caseloads collected in local welfare programs. This information, which is much cruder and more susceptible to local manipulation than that resulting from random-assignment evaluations, is used to monitor local programs, to impose sanctions on programs that are out of compliance with state and federal performance requirements, and in some cases to make local decisions about effectiveness. The only effort to calibrate these local evaluations with random-assignment evaluations—to see, for example, whether local programs with strong results on performance measures also have strong results in random-assignment evaluations—found no correlation between the two (Doolittle and others, 1993, p. 10). This finding suggests that performance measures are virtually useless in making rational decisions about effectiveness, even though they provide political protection because they make JTPA seem like a performance-driven program.

There is little question that the quality of evaluations has increased substantially since the 1970s. Job training programs, particularly those associated with the welfare system, have been the subjects of what is probably the most sophisticated policy-oriented analysis in the United States. But given the complexity of social programs, the variety of job training programs, and the variation in how they are administered in localities in a country as large and diverse as the United States, it should not be surprising that these evaluations have failed to answer all the important questions about job training programs. Therefore, interpretation of the statistical results, of the sort I provide in chapter 6, remains unavoidable.

Chapter 4

The Effectiveness of Job Training Programs: Overall Outcomes

THE LARGE number of evaluations of job training programs performed since the 1970s makes it difficult to summarize them in ways that convey both their findings in a literal sense and the practical importance of the findings. In many cases, job training programs have had statistically significant effects, or benefits that outweigh costs, and therefore appear to be worth doing, but the effects have been so small that they have little real influence on the courses of people's lives, the continuing need for welfare programs, or the future development of those enrolled in youth programs. To convey the findings, I present numerous tables replicating some of the most important and most recent findings, interpret these findings, and summarize early results that are of less interest than recent ones because of the lower quality of the evaluations and because they describe programs no longer in existence.[1]

In this chapter I examine the results of evaluations dealing with the most general effects of job training programs. In the first section I present results for major job training programs, those under the Comprehensive Employment and Training Act and the Job Training Partnership Act. In the second section I present results for welfare-to-work programs and analyze several experimental programs. Chapter 5 examines several questions extending beyond the general effects described here.

Mainstream Job Training Programs: CETA and JTPA

The job training programs that preceded CETA varied widely because of their different funding sources and the great latitude afforded local programs. Partly for this reason, and because the services they offered and the intensity (or duration) of the programs were so diverse, it is difficult to compare evaluations of these early programs. The methodology used in the evaluations varied as well. The earliest evaluations tended to use conventional regression methods involving quasi-experimental control and experimental groups; that is, the researchers would estimate a regression describing earnings (or the log of earnings) as a function of individual characteristics plus a variable describing program participation (or several variables if data were available on the intensity of the program). Table 4.1 summarizes the results (measured by changes in estimated annual earnings) of the evaluations of remedial education and job training programs published from 1962 to 1979 (Taggart, 1981). The table breaks out the results for classroom training, on-the-job training, the Job Corps (a residential, yearlong program for youths that is much more intensive than any other job training program), and adult basic education (ABE), a form of remedial reading and writing instruction. The evaluations found generally positive effects, usually higher for females than for males, of roughly $250–$300 per year (about $900–$1,000 per year in 1994 dollars). However, because of unmeasured selection effects and problems with regression to the mean (discussed in chap. 3), the regression methods used in the studies in table 4.1 cannot possibly control for the probable lower abilities and motivation of those enrolled in programs relative to those not enrolled, so the figures in the table should be considered overestimates of the true effects.

When manpower training programs were consolidated in the CETA program in 1973, the services offered and their administration became somewhat more standardized. In addition, the evaluation of these programs expanded substantially through two different avenues: the Youth Knowledge Development Project, which generated a large number of qualitative studies of CETA programs, and the generation of the Continuous Longitudinal Manpower Survey (CLMS), which followed a random sample of CETA enrollees from 1975 on. CLMS then matched CETA enrollees with comparable individuals from another data set, the Current Population Survey, using different matching methods; then, as in earlier

Table 4.1   Change in Estimated Annual Earnings Found in Pre-CETA Program Evaluations

Program Type and Evaluation	Change (Dollars)	Program Type and Evaluation	Change (Dollars)
Classroom training		*On-the-job-training*	
Ashenfelter, 1978		Cooley, McGuire, and	
Black males	318 to 417	Prescott, 1975	
White males	139 to 322	Males	−38 to 59
Black females	441 to 552	Females	30 to 226
White females	354 to 572	Ketron, Inc., 1979	
Borus, 1964		Minority males	1,984
Males	305	White males	2,181
Borus and Prescott, 1974		Minority females	884
Males	516	White females	926
Females	38	Kiefer, 1976	
Cain and Stromsdorfer, 1968		Black males	−160
White males	828	White males	−61
White females	336	Black females	386
Cooley, McGuire, and		White females	926
Prescott, 1975		Prescott and Cooley, 1972	
Males	71 to 234	Males	796
Females	168 to 291	Sewell, 1971	
Hardin and Borus, 1971	251	Males	375
Ketron, Inc., 1979		Females	754
Minority females	184		
White females	701	*Job Corps*	
Kiefer, 1976		Kiefer, 1976	
Black males	−742 to −355	Black males	−179
White males	−644 to −375	White males	−74
Black females	591	Black females	−188
White females	639	White females	−780
Main, 1968	409	Mallar, 1978	
Page, 1964; Gooding, 1962	446	Males	187
Prescott and Cooley, 1972		Females without children	565
Males	652	Females with children	−206
Sewell, 1971	432		
		Adult basic education	
		Brazzie, 1966	
		Males	2,368
		Roomkin, 1973	
		Males	318
		Females	12

Source: Taggart (1981), table 3.1.

evaluations, regression methods were used to disentangle the effects of personal characteristics (such as gender, race, years of formal education, age, prior labor market experience, and the like) from the effects of program participation.

Table 4.2 presents the results (measured by increases in annual earnings) of several studies that evaluated CETA programs using the CLMS data (Barnow, 1986). The benefits of participation were generally higher for women than for men; indeed, several studies found statistically insignificant effects for men. In general, CETA programs increased earnings for women by about $500–$1,000; whether men's earnings increased is uncertain. For youths, the effects were generally zero or even negative. In addition, a smattering of evidence suggests that classroom training and on-the-job training were more effective than work experience and public service employment, in which individuals were employed in public service jobs at minimal wages; for example, Taggart (1981, p. 282) concluded that classroom training increased earnings in 1976 by $350 or 10 percent; on-the-job training, $850 or 18 percent (declining to $600 the second year); and public service employment, $250 the first year and $350 the second. Individuals in work experience programs actually lost earnings. However, the various studies are too contradictory to give much weight to this result.

The different analyses of the same basic data set were most remarkable for their range of findings: for adult women, the studies showed earnings gains from $0 to $1,300, and for men estimates ranged from an income loss of $700 to a gain of $691. Aside from the powerful selection effects due to the inclusion of only disadvantaged adults, one of the most serious problems in the studies is illustrated in figure 4.1, from Bloom and McLaughlin (1982). The year before enrollment, CETA clients showed a pronounced dip in earnings compared with control group members; that dip is one of the reasons they became eligible for job training. Job training simply restored the level of male earnings to that of the control group but increased female earnings above that of the control group. If the earnings dip is merely a transitory component—caused, for example, by bad luck or a temporary spell of unemployment—then job training programs clearly do nothing for men and have only modest effects for women (about $800–$1,300 in this study, higher than in most others). If, however, the earnings dip was connected to a long-term reduction in earnings capacity, then the benefits of CETA could be considered higher. Disagreement about which of these statements is true is partly responsible

Table 4.2 Change in Estimated Annual Earnings Found in CETA Program Evaluations, by Subgroup (in Dollars)

Evaluation	Subgroup						
	White Women	White Men	Minority Women	Minority Men	Women	Men	All Groups
Westat, Inc., 1981 (FY 1976)	500**	200	600**	200	—	—	300**
Westat, Inc., 1984							
FY 1976	408**	-4	336**	-104	—	—	129**
FY 1977	534**	500**	762**	658**	—	—	596**
Bassi, 1983	740** to 778**	—	426** to 671**	117 to 211	—	—	—
Bassi and others, 1984							
Nonwelfare disadvantaged adults	705** to 762**	17 to 136	779** to 810**	116 to 369	—	—	—
Welfare recipients	840** to 949**	578 to 691**	659** to 703**	-273 to 69	—	—	—
Youths	-68 to -23	-576** to -515**	-201 to -77	-758** to -681**	—	—	—
Bloom and McLaughlin, 1982	—	—	—	—	800** to 1,300**	200	—
Dickinson, Johnson, and West, 1984							
Adults	—	—	—	—	13	-690**	—
Youths	—	—	—	—	185	-591**	—

Source: Barnow (1986), table 3. ** statistically significant at 5 percent.

Figure 4.1   Average Annual Earnings for CETA Participants and Comparison Group Members, 1964–78

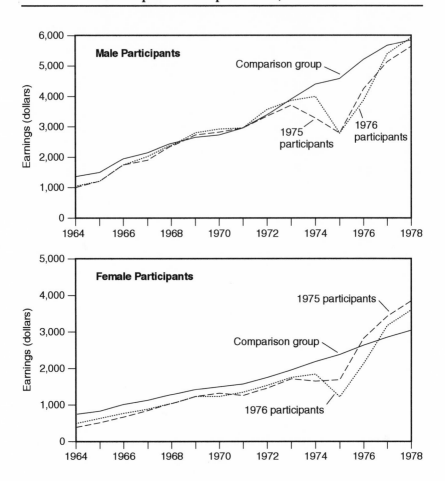

Source: Bloom and McLaughlin (1982), summary figures 1, 2.

for the range of estimates in table 4.2. One conventional conclusion drawn from the range of estimates was that quasi-experimental methods were not powerful enough to detect the possible benefits of job training programs and that the use of experimental methods was advisable (Barnow, 1986). But this conclusion resulted partly from the fact that any benefits from the job training programs must have been modest since even quasi-experimental methods used in substantially different studies would have detected very large benefits.

A special program is the Job Corps, a particularly intensive program for youths. It is predominantly a residential program in which youths live in centers away from home and receive academic instruction, job training, and various other social services for a year. It has always been the most expensive job training program, costing about $15,300 in 1993 dollars (U.S. General Accounting Office, 1995a, p. 7), and has represented the most serious intervention for youths judged in the greatest need. As indicated in table 4.3, a 1980 quasi-experimental evaluation using a matched control group found that the Job Corps had positive effects on employment rates and earnings per week but not on earnings per hour (Mallar and others, 1980). The program has also served to reduce crime among those enrolled. (The finding that earnings per hour did not increase while the amount of employment did suggests that the Job Corps affected persistence in the labor force instead of increasing the productivity of its members, as many other job training programs did.) Furthermore, an early cost-benefit analysis showed that the value of these benefits outweighed the high costs of the Job Corps (Long, Mallar, and Thornton, 1981; see table 5.6) and provided some hope that even intensive job training programs for individuals with the greatest barriers to employment would be worth doing. However, these positive assessments were based on quasi-experimental methods, which tended to upwardly bias the results; recent evidence summarized at the end of this section has cast new doubt on the effectiveness of the Job Corps.

In 1983 CETA, which had come under fire as an ineffective and politically manipulated program, was replaced by JTPA. The two major changes intended to increase effectiveness were the development of performance standards that local programs would be required to meet and the requirement that local administering boards (called Private Industry Councils) draw at least 50 percent of their members from private business, an effort to make job training responsive to the needs of employers. In addition, public service employment, which had been criticized as "make work," was eliminated from the services provided.

With the passage from CETA to JTPA, the evaluations based on CLMS ceased. In their place, a random-assignment evaluation of JTPA was planned (see Bloom and others, 1994). This study, which is widely regarded as definitive because of its design and complexity, describes em-

Table 4.3   Employment and Earnings of 1977 Job Corps and Control Group Participants

Measure and Time since Termination	Job Corps Participants	Control Group	Difference
Fraction of time employed			
0–6 months	.356	.354	.012
6–12 months	.463	.412	.051
12–18 months	.549	.471	.078
18–24 months	.543	.453	.090
Fraction of time in labor force			
0–6 months	.682	.653	.029
6–12 months	.716	.682	.034
12–18 months	.747	.701	.046
18–24 months	.763	.715	.048
Average hours worked a week			
0–6 months	14.46	13.13	1.33
6–12 months	17.82	15.84	1.98
12–18 months	21.55	18.38	3.17
18–24 months	21.39	17.73	3.66
Earnings a week ($)			
0–6 months	45.84	43.82	2.02
6–12 months	64.38	58.38	6.00
12–18 months	82.17	72.48	9.69
18–24 months	21.39	17.73	3.66
Earnings an hour ($)			
0–6 months	3.17	3.37	−0.20
6–12 months	3.61	3.69	−0.08
12–18 months	3.81	3.94	−0.13
18–24 months	3.87	4.16	−0.29

Source: Mallar and others (1980), table 3.6.

ployment effects for individuals from sixteen specific programs across the country both eighteen and thirty months after leaving the program.[2]

Table 4.4 presents the most basic thirty-month results from this evaluation. Like earlier studies on the effects of CETA programs, the study found that JTPA affected adult females (a $1,176, or 9.6 percent, increase in earnings) more than it did adult males (a $978, or 5.3 percent, increase in earnings).[3] However, while these results are statistically significant and

Table 4.4   Earnings of JTPA Participants after Thirty Months, by Target Group

| Target Group | Mean Earnings ($) | | Impact per Assignee | | Impact per Enrollee ($) |
	Assignees and Enrollees	Control Group	$	%	
Adult females	13,417	12,241	1,176***	9.6	1,837***
Adult males	19,474	18,496	978*	5.3	1,599*
Female youths	10,241	10,106	135	1.3	210
Male youth nonarrestees	15,786	16,375	−589	−3.6	−868
Male youth arrestees					
Using survey data	14,633	18,842	−4,209**	−22.3	1,804**
Using scaled UI data	14,148	14,152	−4	0.0	−6

Source: Bloom and others (1994), exhibit 5.
Statistical significance: *** = 1 percent; ** = 5 percent; * = 10 percent. UI stands for unemployment insurance.

while the benefits of JTPA programs proved to outweigh their costs for both adult males and adult females (see table 5.8), in another sense the benefits were small: for women, who might have to support a family, the program increased earnings only from $12,241 to $13,417 over thirty months, an average annual gain of $470. Even for those who enrolled in the program, the increase was only $735 per year—not enough to move individuals out of poverty, for example, or enable them to leave welfare. The long-run effects might be more positive than these, as I explore in chapter 5, but clearly JTPA has not substantially boosted the earnings of either women or men.

Furthermore, the effects of JTPA programs on youths are zero or even negative. The negative findings come about because youths who enroll in a program withdraw from employment during the period of training, and increases in earnings after completing the program do not offset the lower earnings during the period of enrollment. Since labor market experience and a steady work history are among the most important criteria for hiring in the sub-baccalaureate labor market—more important than many educational credentials below the baccalaureate level, as I argue in Grubb (1996)—the long-run effects for youths enrolled in ineffective training programs may be even more negative than the results in table 4.4 show. The negative findings are particularly discouraging for the worst-off youths, those who had been arrested prior to enrolling in the program.

The results for youths in the table reflect only a subset of the youths in JTPA and are therefore not necessarily comprehensive;[4] nonetheless, the discouraging findings confirm in many ways the results of the CETA evaluations shown in table 4.2, and they have caused many analysts and policy makers to call for the elimination of JTPA programs for youths.[5]

Tables 4.5 and 4.6 show three other effects of JTPA. It clearly increased the proportion of individuals earning a general equivalency degree (GED) or high school diploma, though by only trivial amounts for young males, and it reduced the receipt of welfare benefits by female adults and youths (though insignificantly). Unfortunately, it also increased the receipt of welfare benefits among adult males and the arrest rate for young males who had not been arrested prior to enrolling in the program. The positive effects are quite modest and uncertain; furthermore, whether earning a GED (a common measure of outcomes) improves subsequent employment is uncertain.[6] Thus examining benefits other than those related to employment does not improve the conclusions much: benefits exist, but they are modest for some groups, missing for others, and in still other cases, such as the increase in welfare benefits to males and the overall negative effects on youths, they are not benefits at all.

Another evaluation (U.S. General Accounting Office, 1995a) has cast doubt on an early success story, the Job Corps. In that study, only 36 percent of those enrolled completed vocational training, and only half found low-skilled jobs related to their training. Since completers of vocational programs were 50 percent more likely to get a job than noncompleters and were much more likely to get a training-related job, the low rates of completion proved to be a serious limitation. Furthermore, students did not stay with their initial employers very long. One-half worked two months or less, and two years after initial employment 88 percent were no longer working for the same employer: among the predominant reasons, 45 percent had quit, 22 percent were fired, and 13 percent were laid off. These findings apply only to those enrolled in Job Corps, not to any other group, and the focus of Job Corps on severely disadvantaged youths may mean that the results are better than they would have been if the youths had not enrolled in the program, as the results in table 4.3 seem to confirm. But on any absolute scale the employment outcomes are quite dismal, particularly for a program costing over $15,000 per student. Partly because of high costs and partly because of concerns about quality, some of the early support for Job Corps has turned into ambiva-

Table 4.5 Education and AFDC Benefit Levels of JTPA Participants after Thirty Months, by Target Group

| | Percent with GED or High School Diploma | | | | Mean AFDC Benefits ($) | | | |
| | | | Impact (Percentage Points) per | | | | Impact per | |
Target Group	Treatment Group	Control Group	Assignee	Enrollee	Treatment Group	Control Group	Assignee	Enrollee
Adult females	32.0	20.4	11.6**	18.8**	1,972	2,049	−77	−130
Adult males	24.2	16.3	7.9	14.4	258	158	100*	164**
Female youths	39.4	31.7	7.7*	10.6*	1,609	1,734	−125	−193
Male youth nonarrestees	36.8	36.3	0.5	0.7*	158	150	8	12
Male youth arrestees	29.9	28.9	1.0	1.7*	251	69	182	274

Source: Bloom and others (1994), exhibits 8, 9.
Statistical significance: ** = 5 percent; * = 10 percent.

Table 4.6   Arrest Rates of Youths after Participating in JTPA Programs

Follow-up Period and Group	Percent Arrested during Follow-up Period		Impact (Percentage Points) per	
	Treatment Group	Control Group	Assignee	Enrollee
During first follow-up period				
Females	4.4	3.6	0.8	1.3
Male nonarrestees	14.1	9.6	4.5**	6.5**
Male arrestees	43.3	42.6	0.7	1.1
During full follow-up period				
Females	7.0	5.3	1.7	2.7
Male nonarrestees	25.8	18.7	7.1**	10.4**
Male arrestees	59.2	55.7	3.5	5.5

Source: Orr and others (1994), exhibit 4.22.
Statistical significance: ** = 5 percent.

lence, and congressional proposals have sought to cut its funding, though it remains a politically popular program based on the early results.

Overall, the results of these evaluations are sobering. They reveal modest gains in annual earnings for adult men and women, on the order of $400–$650 per year and $500–$750 per year, respectively, but no increases or even losses in income for youths.[7] The results for adults are statistically significant, and JTPA programs are also worth funding in the sense that their benefits outweigh their costs (see chap. 5 and table 5.8). But the benefits are not significant in any practical sense: they are too small to change the life conditions of those who have enrolled in job training, to enable many to leave the welfare rolls, or to escape poverty, and they do not benefit youths at all. And the apparent success of Job Corps in the treatment of youths seems much less certain than it once was. These findings, replicated in many other studies, lead to the puzzling question addressed in chapter 6: after about twenty-five years of development, why are the benefits of job training so small?

Welfare-to-Work Programs

As mentioned in chapter 1, the idea of providing services, including education and training, to enable welfare recipients to move into employment and off welfare dates at least from 1962. In addition to the voluntary work programs established during the 1960s, the federal government under President Richard Nixon allowed states to experiment with their own welfare-to-work programs. Although primitive, to say the least, the evaluations of these programs generated an enormous amount of rhetoric on behalf of welfare-to-work programs. For example, while governor of California, Ronald Reagan established a community work experience program in which welfare recipients were required to work in community service jobs in amounts related to their grants (that is, they were required to "work off" their welfare grants). The California CWEP was a complete failure: it was able to enroll only a tiny fraction (0.2 percent) of welfare recipients, and it failed to meet any of its employment objectives (State of California, 1976). Nonetheless, Reagan—never one to pay undue attention to the evidence—cited the program as a success virtually every time he discussed welfare and used its presumed "success" to press for an expansion of welfare-to-work programs.

While the early welfare-to-work experiments tended to emphasize work rather than education and job training, the emphasis shifted somewhat in the 1980s. During the Reagan administration, states were allowed to implement a series of experiments in their welfare programs that incorporated a mix of work requirements and services (including education and training) designed to reduce their welfare populations. These experiments varied widely, but most emphasized job search rather than either job training or mandatory work; the political and practical difficulties involved in forcing welfare recipients into employment when they had children, deficient skills, and in many cases other personal characteristics that made employment difficult were too great for mandatory work to ever succeed.

As was true of state programs in general, the state welfare-to work programs of the 1980s varied substantially in the services they provided. For example, of the five state programs described in table 4.7, the Arkansas and San Diego programs featured job search workshops followed by work experience in public and private agencies; Virginia's program began with a period of job search followed by either work experience, education, or training; Baltimore's included a variety of different services, including education, training, job search, on-the-job training, and work experience; and West Virginia's required community work experience, potentially of unlimited duration. Like other state programs, these five tended to emphasize job search assistance and work experience programs over education or job training. The services in these welfare-to-work programs overlapped

Table 4.7 Employment and AFDC Benefits of Five State Welfare-to-Work Programs

Program and Measure	Participants	Control Group	Difference	Change (%)
San Diego applicants				
Ever employed during 15 months (%)	61.0	55.4	5.6***	10
Average total earnings during 15 months ($)	3,802	3,102	700***	23
Ever received AFDC payments during 18 months (%)	83.9	84.3	−0.4	0
Average months receiving AFDC payments during 18 months	8.13	8.61	−0.48*	−6
Average total AFDC payments received during 18 months ($)	3,409	3,697	−288**	−8
Baltimore applicants and recipients				
Ever employed during 12 months (%)	51.2	44.2	7.0***	16
Average total earnings during 12 months ($)	1,935	1,759	176	10
Ever received AFDC payments during 15 months (%)	94.9	95.1	−0.2	0
Average months receiving AFDC payments during 15 months	11.14	11.29	−0.15	−1
Average total AFDC payments received during 15 months ($)	3,058	3,064	−6	0

Arkansas applicants and recipients			
Ever employed during 6 months (%)	18.8	14.0	4.8**	34
Average total earnings during 6 months ($)	291	213	78*	37
Ever received AFDC payments during 9 months (%)	72.8	75.9	-3.1	-4
Average months receiving AFDC payments during 9 months	4.96	5.49	-0.53***	-10
Average total AFDC payments received during 9 months ($)	772	865	-93***	-11
Virginia applicants and recipients			
Ever employed during 9 months (%)	43.8	40.5	3.3*	8
Average total earnings during 9 months ($)	1,119	1,038	81	8
Ever received AFDC payments during 12 months (%)	86.0	86.1	-0.1	0
Average months receiving AFDC payments during 12 months	7.75	7.90	-0.14	-2
Average total AFDC payments received during 12 months ($)	1,923	2,007	-84**	-4
West Virginia applicants and recipients			
Ever employed during 15 months (%)	22.3	22.7	-0.4	-2
Average total earnings during 15 months ($)	713	712	0	0
Ever received AFDC payments during 21 months (%)	96.8	96.0	0.8	1
Average months receiving AFDC payments during 21 months	14.26	14.46	-0.21	-1
Average total AFDC payments received during 21 months ($)	2,681	2,721	-40	-1

Source: Gueron (1987), table 2.
Statistical significance: *** = 10 percent; ** = 5 percent; * = 1 percent.

those provided by JTPA, but the evaluations of these experiments should not be considered evaluations of training itself.

The five state welfare-to-work programs described above were evaluated with random-assignment methods (Gueron, 1987; see table 4.7). The results were revealing, and they set the stage for more widespread programs enacted in 1988. Four of the five increased the amount of employment, two increased earnings by statistically significant amounts ($560 per year in San Diego and $156 per year in Arkansas), and two increased earnings by amounts that were not quite statistically significant ($176 per year in Baltimore and $108 per year in Virginia). As a result, in three of the five states recipients' total welfare payments per year decreased by amounts ranging from $84 in Virginia to $192 in San Diego. But in none of these five states did the program reduce the likelihood of being on welfare.[8]

These evaluations of the five state programs formed the basis for a number of other useful conclusions in addition to dispelling the notion that "nothing works." The least effective program was that of West Virginia, but the poor results were generally attributed to the weak economy in a largely rural state with few employment prospects. This result suggested that welfare-to-work programs (and job training programs in general) could not be expected to have much effect in weak economies, and perhaps in rural economies generally. Second, the state experimental programs appeared to provide the most help to the poorest or the least job-ready individuals—to help women more than men and individuals without prior employment more than those with a work history (Gueron, 1987). Taken together with similar results from CETA program evaluations, these results suggested that job training programs ought to concentrate their efforts on individuals with the most barriers to employment—the very opposite of "creaming."

The welfare-to-work experiments yielded benefits of some kind in virtually all states, and the benefits exceeded the costs of operating these programs (see chap. 5 and table 5.7). In addition, the benefits varied among states, and the San Diego experience suggested that earnings increases could be substantial—at least on the order of the magnitude of the benefits recorded by JTPA. However, the effects were still modest by almost any standard: earnings increases were quite small, between $100 and $200 per year in most states; the reductions in welfare payments by states were similarly small; and the programs did not reduce the number of families on the welfare rolls, the goal at the heart of welfare-to-work programs. The results, which could be read as either supporting or un-

Table 4.8   Effects of Massachusetts ET Choices Program on Employment, Earnings, and AFDC Participation

	Participants	Control Group	Difference	Change (%)
Probability of employment (%)	44.5	36.3	8.2***	23
Six-month earnings ($)	1,537	1,147	390***	34
Duration of current AFDC spell (months)	10.21	14.44	−4.23***	−29
Average monthly AFDC grant ($)	294.40	320	−25.60***	−8

Source: Nightingale and others (1991), tables 4.1, 4.2, 4.3, 4.4, and associated text.
Statistical significance: *** = 1 percent.

dermining the continuation of welfare-to-work programs, indicated that such efforts made very little difference in the lives of welfare recipients and provided only trivial savings for taxpayers.

An evaluation of a state welfare-to-work program, the Massachusetts Employment and Training (ET) Choices program, used a nonexperimental design (Nightingale and others, 1991). The study evaluated the program by comparing ET Choices participants with a control group of other welfare recipients who did not participate but who were matched on the basis of race or ethnicity, age, sex, the age of the youngest child in the recipient's family, the region of the state in which the recipient lived, and the type of family (one- or two-parent). Regression methods controlled for variations among individuals (and between the experimental and comparison groups). The results, summarized in table 4.8, are of the same order of magnitude as the experimental results in table 4.7 but are somewhat more positive: the probability of employment increased more than in the five state programs described in table 4.7, average annual earnings increased more ($780), and annual welfare payments decreased by an amount ($307) larger than the largest reduction achieved by the five state programs ($192 per year for the San Diego program). It is difficult to know whether these differences are due to variation among states (that is, whether Massachusetts simply had a better program), to the greater variety of services offered in ET Choices (which allowed welfare recipients to enroll in job training, postsecondary education, and remedial education in addition to job search assistance and supported work experience), or to the nonexperimental design of the evaluation, which probably resulted in outcomes that were upwardly biased. However, the results confirm once again that welfare-to-work programs can affect both earnings and welfare grants, though the effects are modest and even under favorable conditions are unable either to improve the lives of welfare recipients substantially or to end the need for welfare itself.

In 1988, in part based on a favorable reading of the experimental program evaluations, the early welfare-to-work programs were expanded in the Job Opportunities and Basic Skills program. JOBS required states to fund welfare-to-work programs (partly with federal matching funds) with a mix of work requirements, job search assistance, work experience, training, education, counseling, child care, and other supportive services. Again, states set up programs that differed in job requirements and mix of services, which included job training, education, and less intensive services like job search assistance. However, many states implemented their JOBS programs through JTPA as a matter of state policy, while other states convened a variety of local providers of JOBS programs and emphasized the use of the existing JTPA system, in effect commingling JOBS and the dominant job training system.[9]

So far, two evaluations of JOBS programs have been completed: one of the California program, called GAIN (Greater Avenues for Independence), and another of the Florida program, Project Independence. The GAIN evaluation, using random-assignment methods, investigated the effects of programs in six counties (of fifty-eight) that differed in urban and rural characteristics, the state of the local labor market, and the nature of local programs (Riccio, Friedlander, and Freedman, 1994). Of the many services GAIN provided, enrollees increased most their use of job search activities (used by 28.5 percent of the experimental group and 3.9 percent of the control group) and remedial education (defined as ABE or GED training, received by 29 percent of the experimental group and 5.4 percent of the control group), but vocational training and postsecondary education did not increase markedly as a result of GAIN. This finding confirms a bias within welfare-to-work programs: even though welfare recipients are allowed to participate in self-initiated education and job training programs lasting up to two years, in practice the emphasis on short-term job search assistance and on remedial education has reduced the use of lengthier education and training programs.[10]

The overall results are summarized in table 4.9 and differentiated into effects for single parents (almost all women) and heads of two-parent families (almost all men). Over the three-year period of the evaluation (from early 1988 to mid-1990) the program increased the probability of employment for both groups; increased earnings for both groups, by $471 per

Table 4.9 Earnings, AFDC Benefits, Employment, and Education after Participation in GAIN

	Participants	Control Group	Difference	Change (%)
Single parents				
Earnings over three years ($)	7,781	6,367	1,414***	22
Total AFDC payments ($)	14,464	15,426	−916***	−6
Ever employed in year 3 (%)	39.6	33.7	5.9***	—
On AFDC in last quarter of year 3 (%)	52.5	55.5	−3.0***	—
Received GED or high school diploma (%)	7.2	1.9	5.4	—
Received trade certificate (%)	9.2	8.8	0.4	—
Heads of two-parent families				
Earnings over three years ($)	10,156	9,045	1,111***	12
Total AFDC payments ($)	18,164	19,332	−1,168***	−6
Ever employed in year 3 (%)	44.6	40.1	4.5***	—
On AFDC in last quarter of year 3 (%)	57.3	57.7	−0.5	—

Source: Riccio, Friedlander, and Freedman (1994), tables 1, 2, 8, 9, 2.9.
Statistical significance: *** = 1 percent.

year and $370, respectively; and reduced the amount of welfare payments, by $305 per year and $389, respectively. GAIN also reduced the likelihood of being on welfare by 3 percentage points among the single parents (55.5 percent of the control group but only 52.5 percent of the experimental group was on welfare at the end of the third year);[11] however, the program did not move heads of households off welfare. These effects represent averages across all six counties; the substantial variation among counties (reviewed in chap. 5) indicated that GAIN programs in some counties were more effective than others. Overall, however, the results are quite consistent with the pre-JOBS results: welfare-to-work programs relying on the most modest services—in this case, job search assistance and remediation—can increase employment and earnings and result in some welfare savings, but the effects are small and the reduction in the numbers of families on welfare is trivial.

The results from Project Independence are different in several respects (Kemple, Friedlander, and Fellerath, 1995). This welfare-to-work program was really a job search program that provided relatively little education or training. Like many other programs, it increased the amount of

Table 4.10   Employment and Earnings after Two Years in Project Independence

Cohort, Outcome, and Follow-up Period	Participants	Control Group	Difference	Change (%)
Total cohort				
Ever employed (%)				
Years 1–2	66.3	63.8	2.5***	4.0
Year 1	55.4	52.6	2.8***	5.4
Year 2	53.3	51.2	2.1***	4.1
Year 2, last quarter	38.3	37.8	0.4	1.1
Average total earnings ($)				
Years 1–2	5,766	5,539	227*	4.1
Year 1	2,548	2,401	146**	6.1
Year 2	3,219	3,138	80	2.6
Ever received AFDC payments (%)				
Years 1–2	88.3	89.5	−1.1**	−1.3
Year 1, last quarter	64.6	68.7	−4.2***	−6.0
Year 2, last quarter	51.2	53.6	−2.4***	−4.5
Average total AFDC payments received ($)				
Years 1–2	4,028	4,293	−265***	−6.2
Year 1	2,196	2,348	−152***	−6.5
Year 2	1,832	1,945	−113***	−5.8
Early cohort				
Average total earnings ($)				
Years 1–2	5,619	5,180	439**	8.5
Year 1	2,499	2,283	216**	9.5
Year 2	3,120	2,897	223*	7.7
Year 3	3,538	3,261	277*	8.5
Average total AFDC payments received ($)				
Years 1–2	4,003	4,244	−241***	−5.7
Year 1	2,115	2,240	−125***	−5.6
Year 2	1,889	2,004	−115***	−5.7
Year 3	1,438	1,503	−65	−4.3

Source: Kemple, Friedlander, and Fellerath (1995), tables 3, 6.2, 6.4.
Statistical significance: *** = 1 percent; ** = 5 percent; * = 10 percent.

both employment and earnings (table 4.10), although the average increase of $114 per year was very small. It also succeeded in reducing the rate at which individuals received welfare. In fact, the reductions in welfare payments were greater than the increases in earnings, a finding that affects the cost-benefit analysis substantially (see table 5.10). Two other findings

Table 4.10   *(continued)*

Cohort, Outcome, and Follow-up Period	Participants	Control Group	Difference	Change (%)
Late cohort				
Average total earnings ($)				
Years 1–2	5,873	5,774	99	1.7
Year 1	2,584	2,473	111	4.5
Year 2	3,289	3,301	−12	−0.4
Average total AFDC payments received ($)				
Years 1–2	4,043	4,333	−289***	−6.7
Year 1	2,253	2,426	−173***	−7.1
Year 2	1,791	1,907	−116***	−6.1
Youngest child aged 6 or older				
Average total earnings ($)				
Years 1–2	6,228	5,755	473**	8.2
Year 1	2,790	2,506	284***	11.3
Year 2	3,438	3,249	190	5.8
Average total AFDC payments received ($)				
Years 1–2	3,720	4,024	−304***	−7.5
Year 1	2,053	2,224	−171***	−7.7
Year 2	1,667	1,800	−133***	−7.4
Youngest child aged 3–5				
Average total earnings ($)				
Years 1–2	5,202	5,183	20	0.4
Year 1	2,268	2,214	54	2.4
Year 2	2,935	2,969	−34	−1.1
Average total AFDC payments received ($)				
Years 1–2	4,467	4,677	−210***	−4.5
Year 1	2,405	2,538	−133***	−5.2
Year 2	2,062	2,139	−77*	−3.6

were of greater interest. The evaluation found much higher benefits for mothers with children over the age of six, who have many fewer problems related to child care, scheduling, sick days, and the like, than for mothers with children aged three to five (see table 4.10). This finding reinforces the notion that individuals with substantial barriers to employment may not benefit from job training, an idea examined further in chapter 5.

The evaluation of Project Independence revealed a vulnerability common to job training and welfare programs. During the evaluation, a worsening recession in Florida caused welfare caseloads to increase while funding stayed the same; the result was that the resources available to clients who enrolled late in the evaluation—the late cohort in table 4.10—were substantially smaller than for the early cohort. Consistent with this circumstance, the increases in earnings and the declines in welfare payments were significant for the early cohort, for whom earnings increased 8.5 percent, but not for the late cohort, for whom earnings increased an insignificant 1.7 percent. The difference in the increases clarifies the notion that the fiscal conditions of the regions surrounding welfare-to-work programs may influence the outcomes substantially. The implication is that individuals who point to exemplary welfare-to-work programs as evidence of what job training might accomplish (for example, the Riverside program described in chapter 5 and table 5.5) neglect the greater likelihood that fiscal constraints will lead to low-quality programs without substantial effects.

One hint of how Project Independence affected the behavior of participants came from an examination of attitudes and values. Those who enrolled in the program were more likely than nonparticipants to agree that "even a low-paying job is better than being on welfare," were less likely to think that mothers should stay home with their children instead of working, and had lower reservation wages. Even though many of these differences were statistically insignificant, they all support the notion that welfare-to-work programs can change attitudes by replacing an acceptance of welfare with a greater commitment to work—a finding consistent with one of the intentions behind welfare-to-work programs. But Project Independence also reduced the overall income of those enrolled by a small amount, and it decreased the fraction of enrollees saying that they were satisfied or very satisfied with their overall standard of living from 45.7 percent among the control group to 41.9 percent among those in the program. Project Independence therefore represents a relatively conservative approach to welfare-to-work programs, in which the cost of welfare to taxpayers declines (see table 5.10) at the expense of welfare recipients themselves, who were arguably worse off as a result of the program. What the long-run effects will be for the enrollees' children, who are, after all, the intended beneficiaries of Aid to Families with Dependent Children, remains unknown.

One final set of results is interesting but still inconclusive. In addition to the evaluations of the California and Florida welfare-to-work programs, the Department of Health and Human Services is currently funding an evaluation of JOBS programs in seven sites around the United States. Early results are available for programs in three sites: Atlanta, Georgia; Grand Rapids, Michigan; and Riverside, California (Freedman and Friedlander, 1995). A central objective of this evaluation has been to determine the relative effectiveness of two broad strategies: one, labeled *labor force attachment*, emphasizes job search assistance, perhaps along with work experience or short-term training to get individuals into jobs quickly, and the other, labeled *human capital development*, provides longer-term education and training so that clients can develop more substantial skills than they can under the labor force attachment strategy. One might expect the short-run effects of labor force attachment strategies to be greater than those of the human capital development approach, which requires individuals to be out of the labor force for longer periods of time. However, the long-term effects of these two strategies might be quite different, subject either to the decline of initial positive effects (see chap. 5) or to sustained positive effects.

Unfortunately, the results available after two years of evaluation are too preliminary to clarify the long-run effects of the two strategies, though they are roughly consistent with expectations of what they might accomplish in the short run. As summarized in table 4.11, the labor force attachment approach did succeed in increasing the amount of employment and earnings, although the magnitude of these effects, while large in percentage terms (a 25.8 percent increase in earnings, for example), was in practical terms insubstantial (earnings increased from only $2,712 per year to $3,420, still well below the poverty line). Because of the earnings increase, the amount of welfare and food stamps benefits fell, so that recipients were slightly worse off than the control group. As one might expect, the human capital development approach did not increase earnings during the first two years, since clients were in education and training activities, and reduced welfare payments, so that in the short run recipients were worse off. These results, like those of Project Independence (table 4.10), indicate what welfare advocates have always feared about welfare-to-work programs: under certain conditions they may save taxpayers money, but they do so by making families with children who are dreadfully poor to start with even poorer.

Experimental Programs

A common pattern in the United States has been to experiment with social programs by trying out promising practices on a small scale before expanding them to larger, universal programs. Indeed, the history of job

Table 4.11   Income Sources for Single Parents after Two Years in the JOBS Program

	Participants	Control Group	Difference	Change (%)
Labor force attachment approach				
Percent with income from				
Employment	42.5	34.4	8.1***	23.5
Employment with earnings equivalent to at least $10,000 per year	13.7	9.8	3.8**	39.0
AFDC	57.2	68.3	−11.1***	−16.2
Food stamps	65.1	73.3	−8.2***	−11.2
Percent covered by Medicaid or private health insurance	77.4	82.7	−5.3***	−6.4
Average amount received from ($)				
Earnings	285	226	58***	25.8
AFDC	216	276	−61***	−21.9
Food stamps	132	153	−21***	−13.7
Total income (from these and other sources)	682	701	−19	−2.7
Sample size (*N*)	759	951		
Human capital development approach				
Percent with income from				
Employment	35.1	32.4	2.6	8.1
Employment with earnings equivalent to at least $10,000 per year	8.0	9.1	−1.1	−11.8
AFDC	64.6	68.8	−4.2**	−6.1
Food stamps	72.7	74.5	−1.9	−2.5
Percent covered by Medicaid or private health insurance	79.2	81.8	−2.6	−3.2
Average amount received from ($)				
Earnings	207	209	−2	−0.8
AFDC	247	285	−38***	−13.5
Food stamps	151	156	−5	−3.3
Total income (from these and other sources)	653	697	−44**	−6.3
Sample size (*N*)	894	828		

Source: Freedman and Friedlander (1995), table ES-1.
Note: All values refer to levels the month before the survey.
Statistical significance: *** = 1 percent; ** = 5 percent.

training efforts can be interpreted as part of this larger history. The development in the 1960s of manpower training programs located outside the schools was in part an effort to develop novel efforts that bypassed the presumed deficiencies of the educational system; these "experiments," with the roughly positive results summarized in table 4.1, were institutionalized in CETA and then in JTPA. Similarly, the current round of welfare-to-work programs under JOBS emerged from welfare-to-work experiments operated by states during the 1980s, which were in turn based on the fledgling efforts of the 1960s and 1970s.

Several other, more self-consciously experimental programs developed with private and foundation funding have contributed to the knowledge of what works in job training programs. The number of experimental programs, each with its partisans, has been quite large, partly because private foundations in the United States often operate by developing an experimental approach (or discovering an experimental approach under way in some corner of the country) and then replicating it elsewhere, often after some kind of evaluation. A few of these programs have proved not especially effective because they cannot be replicated; for example, some are dependent on the high energy and charisma of a founding leader and do not work once other people operate them. However, others have been designed to be replicated and are intended to be tests of particular approaches to employment and training. In contrast to the mainstream job training and welfare-to-work programs, which have provided a variety of services often without much thought or guidance about what might be appropriate, these experimental programs have developed clear models of what employment-related services ought to be provided to specific population groups and have worked to implement these models carefully. One might therefore expect these experimental programs to be of higher quality and to generate more favorable outcomes than do the mainstream programs reviewed in the previous two sections.

In this section I present the evidence on the effects of four experimental programs: two for young mothers with children, the Minority Female Single Parent (MFSP) Demonstration and New Chance; and two for youths, JOBSTART for high school dropouts and the Summer Training and Employment Program (STEP) for youths at risk of dropping out of high school.

The Minority Female Single Parent Demonstration

The MFSP Demonstration was an effort to devise an effective employment program for a group that has special difficulties in gaining access to stable employment and is likely to be on welfare for long periods of time: minority women with children but without husbands. The program, which took place in four sites, emphasized the provision of remedial education, on the assumption that deficiencies in basic academic skills were a barrier to employment, and provided an extensive array of services like child care, counseling, guidance in managing daily problems, and help in finding jobs after the program. Two programs (the Atlanta Urban League [AUL] and the Opportunities Industrialization Center [OIC] in Rhode Island) emphasized classroom courses in academic skills along with job-specific training; one (the Center for Employment Training [CET] in San Jose, California) supposedly emphasized very specific job-skill training; and Wider Opportunities for Women (WOW) in Baltimore emphasized skills that increase general employability (including basic academic competencies as well as communications skills, motivation, and discipline) through classroom activities (Gordon and Burghardt, 1990; Rangarajan, Burghardt, and Gordon, 1992). The MFSP Demonstration, funded partly by foundations, was evaluated with random-assignment methods.

Because the four MFSP Demonstration sites offered somewhat different services, the outcomes were reported separately for each of the four programs. Table 4.12 presents the most important results. Three of the four programs had no influence whatsoever on employment and earnings or the receipt of welfare benefits over the period of the evaluation. However, one program, CET, increased average monthly hours of employment 13 percent; average earnings 25 percent, or $101 per month ($1,212 annually); and wage rates 11 percent—huge effects compared with those of the JTPA programs presented in table 4.4, for example, or of GAIN presented in table 4.9. Like GAIN and earlier welfare-to-work programs, the MFSP Demonstration neither decreased welfare payments substantially nor decreased the likelihood of being on welfare.

The MFSP Demonstration results can be read either positively or negatively. On the negative side, three of four carefully designed programs failed to have any effects at all. On the positive side, the substantial effects of CET, confirmed in the JOBSTART evaluation reviewed below, suggested that well-designed programs can work. Indeed, the success of the CET program in this evaluation has been the subject of a publicity campaign to trumpet the success of a particular approach. The evaluators and the founder, who believed that the success of CET was due to its efforts to integrate remedial education and vocational skill training, began to promote a model of job training that depends on such an integration

Table 4.12 Average Employment and Earnings, Public Assistance, and Training Levels of MFSP Demonstration Participants, Quarters 7–10 after Application

| | MFSP Demonstration Program | | | | | | | | | | |
| | Atlanta Urban League | | | Center for Employment Training | | | Opportunities Industrialization Center | | | Wider Opportunities for Women | | |
Outcome	Participants	Control Group	Difference	Participants	Control Group	Difference	Participants	Control Group	Difference	Participants	Control Group	Difference
Employment and earnings												
Monthly employment rate (%)	50.9	49.7	1.2	46.1	42.0	4.1	37.9	38.9	−1.1	54.8	49.7	5.1**
Monthly hours	76.1	75.7	0.4	73.3	65.0	8.2	54.9	58.0	−3.1	83.8	77.2	6.6
Monthly earnings ($)	432	425	6	506	405	101**	343	323	20	520	477	43
Hourly wage ($)	5.56	5.35	0.21	6.65	6.01	0.64**	5.79	5.55	0.24	5.95	5.95	0.0
Public assistance and total income												
Percent receiving welfare	50.2	51.4	−1.2	48.3	49.6	−1.3	66.7	64.4	2.3	42.7	45.8	−3.1
Monthly welfare income ($)	198	210	−12	284	318	−34	368	369	−1	186	208	−23
Earnings ($)	442	427	15	551	450	101**	376	354	22	553	515	38
Monthly income ($)	697	699	−1	885	832	53	796	792	4	786	788	−3
Training												
Percent in training	24.2	15.1	9.1***	22.7	14.7	8.0***	31.6	14.8	16.8	21.4	15.8	5.6
Percent working or in training	61.2	53.7	7.5***	60.2	48.5	11.7***	55.7	41.4	14.3	59.1	54.6	4.5

Sources: Gordon and Burghardt (1990), table 4.1; Rangarajan, Burghardt, and Gordon (1992), tables IV.1, V.1, V.4.
Statistical significance: *** = 1 percent; ** = 5 percent.

(Burghardt and Gordon, 1990; see also Rockefeller Foundation and Wider Opportunities for Women, 1989). This approach may in fact be worthwhile, as I argue in chapter 7, but the success of CET is due to many factors in addition to the provision of both remediation and job-skill training, as I point out in chapter 5.

Overall, however, the results of the MFSP Demonstration are remarkably consistent with those of other evaluations, especially those of GAIN: job training programs on the average have modest positive effects on employment and earnings, very little effect if any on welfare payments, and no effect on the likelihood of being on welfare, although individual programs (like CET) may have much more substantial effects.[12]

New Chance

The New Chance program was an experiment conducted between 1989 and 1992 at sixteen sites in ten states. Similar to the MFSP Demonstration, it concentrated on young mothers, almost all high school dropouts. The New Chance model assumed that poor young mothers require a range of supportive services in addition to remedial education and job training because they are faced with a variety of personal and psychological barriers to employment. The sites provided remedial education, preparation for the GED, career exploration, health education, and instruction in job-finding skills, family planning, and life skills; a second phase offered more employment-focused services, including job training, work experience, and job placement assistance. New Chance also offered child care and some services to children, including heath care. Services were more intensive than the usual JTPA or JOBS services and were scheduled for twenty to thirty hours per week for up to eighteen months.

Table 4.13 presents the findings of random-assignment evaluations performed eighteen months after the experimental group entered the program (Quint and others, 1994). (Subsequent results will examine results after forty-two months; if positive results emerge only after a period longer than eighteen months, they will not be apparent in the findings presented here.) New Chance was successful in increasing attendance in GED programs and college and in the proportion of mothers who earned a GED and some credits toward a postsecondary credential. Surprisingly, however, the program did not increase scores on a test of basic skills (the Test of Adult Basic Education, or TABE), and 72 percent of those enrolling (compared with 70.2 percent of the controls) left the program reading at

Table 4.13   Outcomes for Low-Income Mothers after Eighteen Months in the New Chance Program

Outcome	Participants	Control Group	Difference
Participation rate (%)			
Any education program	85.3	60.4	24.9***
Basic education/GED	79.4	47.1	32.4***
High school	2.5	3.6	−1.1
College	12.5	7.9	4.6***
Other education	20.1	17.8	2.3
Skills training or unpaid work	35.2	23.3	11.8***
Skills training	33.3	22.5	10.8***
Unpaid work	6.3	2.2	4.1***
Education (%)			
Earned GED or high school diploma	43.1	30.0	13.1***
Earned GED	36.8	21.1	15.8***
Earned high school diploma	6.6	9.2	−2.6***
Earned trade certificate or license	12.5	12.4	0.1
Earned credits toward associate or baccalaureate degree	9.8	7.1	2.6**
Average TABE reading score	748.7	748.3	0.4
Fertility (%)			
Pregnant	57.0	53.0	4.0*
Had given birth	28.4	26.2	2.2
Had had an abortion	14.9	11.1	3.8*
Sexually abstinent, not pregnant	17.8	19.5	−1.7
Sexually active, contracepting regularly	37.0	41.0	−4.0*
Sexually active, not contracepting regularly	30.2	25.2	4.9**
Employment			
Ever employed, months 1–8 (%)	42.6	44.9	−2.2
Average number of weeks employed in months 1–18	9.1	10.8	−1.8**
Average earnings in months 1–18 ($)	1,366	1,708	−342**
Receiving welfare at 18 months (%)	82.1	81.5	0.7
Average total income in month prior to follow-up interview ($)	802	799	3

Source: Quint and others (1994), tables 3–6.
Statistical significance: *** = 1 percent; ** = 5 percent; * = 10 percent.

a ninth-grade level or below, suggesting that it is possible to earn a GED without improving academic competencies.[13]

For a wide range of other outcomes, however, New Chance made no difference in enrollees' lives in the short run. Indeed, it appeared to have *negative* consequences if any: to increase pregnancies, though they were balanced by increased abortions so that the number of births stayed about the same; to reduce employment; to reduce earnings significantly; and to increase welfare received slightly. These results may reflect withdrawal from employment during the period of the program itself, and early declines in employment and earnings may reverse after young women get into more stable employment in their third and fourth years after enrolling (as in the JOBSTART program, summarized below). However, the early findings, roughly consistent with the MFSP Demonstration results, are not at all encouraging since the only real benefit has been an increase in a credential, the GED, that has little effect on either employment or subsequent education. The results are particularly discouraging in view of the high cost of the program: about $9,000 per enrollee.

JOBSTART

The JOBSTART program was an experimental effort to create effective programs for youths aged seventeen to twenty-one who have dropped out of high school. While high school dropout rates have been considered a problem in the United States virtually throughout this century, recently the problem has become even more serious because the employment and earnings of dropouts have been falling relative to those of high school completers (Grubb and Wilson, 1992; Levy and Murnane, 1992) and because dropouts constitute a majority of the population that is permanently poor or on welfare (as distinct from those who are poor or receive welfare payments only temporarily). Conventional job training programs for youths have not been successful, as the results of the JTPA evaluation in table 4.4 illustrate quite starkly, although these dismal results were not available when JOBSTART was initiated in 1985.

The JOBSTART Demonstration, which used JTPA funds, took place in thirteen sites in the United States; it was modeled roughly on the apparently successful Job Corps program but was less intensive and nonresidential. Each site provided remedial education, vocational skill training, job placement assistance, and various support services like child care, transportation, counseling, and instruction in work readiness and job skills; sites were required to offer at least two hundred hours of basic education and five hundred hours of job training, making the programs more intensive than conventional JTPA programs. JOBSTART programs followed one of three different models of service provision: concurrent programs provided remedial education and occupational training at the same time; sequential/in-house programs provided remedial education followed by vocational skill training; and sequential/brokered programs provided remedial education and then referred participants to other programs for vocational skill training.

The JOBSTART Demonstration was evaluated using random-assignment methods over a four-year period (Cave and others, 1993). The most important results are summarized in table 4.14. One major result is that the program increased the rate at which dropouts received a GED, which is not surprising because most programs emphasized the GED. However, the limited effects of the GED in increasing employment or access to postsecondary education reduce the value of this accomplishment. Indeed, over the four-year period the effects on employment and earnings were insignificant both for the total sample and for selected subgroups. As in other programs, the proportion of women receiving welfare did not decrease overall—indeed, it increased for women with children—and the amount of welfare payments received did not decrease. Nor did rates of pregnancy or giving birth fall significantly, a special concern because of the negative effect childbearing has on poverty and welfare dependency; indeed, for mothers entering JOBSTART, rates of pregnancy and giving birth *increased* during the program. One positive result is that rates of arrest appeared to fall, as did drug use (significantly so for hard drugs excluding marijuana).

The dismal results in table 4.14 suggest that well-designed job training programs of moderate cost do not work for youths at all. However, these average effects mask some potentially positive findings for the long run. A common pattern was for employment and earnings to fall in the first year of the program, while individuals were enrolled in education and job training, but for employment to increase in the second year and for both employment and earnings to increase in the third and fourth years. This pattern (from the total earnings section of table 4.14), which suggests that those enrolled in the programs increased their earnings about $400 per year over the long run, emerged for most subgroups, including men, mothers, and other women, and was particularly marked for men arrested before enrolling in JOBSTART, whose earnings increased $1,129 in year

Table 4.14   Outcomes for JOBSTART Participants after Four Years

Outcome	Participants	Control Group	Difference
All participants			
Received GED or high school diploma			
(end of year 4) (%)			
Full sample	42.0	28.6	13.4***
Men	42.0	28.3	13.7***
Custodial mothers	42.0	26.7	15.3***
Other women	41.6	31.3	10.4**
Ever employed (%)			
Years 1-4	86.4	86.0	0.4
Year 1	56.5	60.8	−4.3**
Year 2	71.0	67.5	3.5*
Year 3	61.8	61.5	0.3
Year 4	65.7	64.5	1.3
Hours worked			
Years 1–4	3,031	3,071	−40
Year 1	441	550	−109***
Year 2	760	775	−15
Year 3	899	855	44
Year 4	930	890	40
Earnings ($)			
Years 1–4	17,010	16,796	214
Year 1	2,097	2,596	−499***
Year 2	3,991	4,112	−121
Year 3	5,329	4,906	423
Year 4	5,592	5,182	410

Source: Cave and others (1993), tables 2-7.
Statistical significance: *** = 1 percent; ** = 5 percent; * = 10 percent.

3 and $1,872 (and statistically significant) in year 4, and for youths who left school for academic reasons, whose earnings increased $726 in year 3 (statistically significant) and $592 in year 4. In addition, the finding that drug use decreased as a result of the programs suggests that more positive effects might show up in the long run as some individuals avoid drug-related arrests and drug-motivated unemployment and create stable employment records instead.

The other positive finding is that enrollees at one of the thirteen sites— CET in San Jose, the successful MFSP Demonstration site—had statistically significant increases in earnings: over the four-year period, the experimental group earned $32,959 compared with $26,244 for the control group, an increase of 25.6 percent and $1,679 per year (and $3,044 per

Table 4.14 *(continued)*

Outcome	Participants	Control Group	Difference
Custodial mothers (years 1–4)			
Ever employed (%)	75.4	71.0	4.5
Total earnings ($)	8,959	8,334	625
Ever received AFDC (%)	84.8	81.6	3.2
Total AFDC income ($)	9,371	9,334	37
Ever pregnant (%)	76.1	67.5	8.6**
Ever gave birth (%)	67.8	57.9	9.9**
Other women (years 1–4)			
Ever employed (%)	84.3	85.3	−1.0
Total earnings ($)	13,923	13,310	613
Ever received AFDC (%)	38.0	45.1	−7.1
Total AFDC income ($)	3,204	3,979	−775
Ever pregnant (%)	64.4	65.6	−1.2
Ever gave birth (%)	52.7	56.5	−3.9
Men			
Ever employed, years 1–4 (%)	94.1	94.5	−0.4
Total earnings, years 1–4 ($)	23,364	23,637	−273
Ever arrested (%)			
Year 1	35.1	35.1	−0.1
Years 1–4	68.9	74.8	−5.8
Ever used any drug, year 4 (%)	25.4	31.0	−5.5
Ever used any drug excluding marijuana, year 4 (%)	3.7	10.5	−6.9*
Ever used marijuana, year 4 (%)	25.3	30.2	−4.9

year over years 3 and 4). Unfortunately, disaggregating by sites makes the findings more dismal, if anything. Seven of the thirteen sites had *negative* outcomes (about what one would expect by chance alone), and two of them had very large negative effects in the range of $6,200 over the four years. If the one clear success of CET is eliminated as a special case, the other twelve sites averaged *negative* effects of $1,393 over four years and $211 over years 3 and 4, making it difficult to conclude that the long-run effects could be positive. The CET program may be a success story, for special reasons I analyze in chapter 5, but otherwise it is difficult to find much hope for youth programs in the JOBSTART results.

Summer Training and Employment Program

The Summer Training and Employment Program is an interesting effort to devise a coherent program for youths in their junior and senior years of high school (that is, those who have not yet dropped out, as JOBSTART youths had) but who were considered to be likely to drop out because of their poor academic performance or, if female, to become pregnant. STEP was designed to combat the problem of "summer effects"—the fact that the academic achievement of many youths (especially low-income youths) regresses during the summer. Therefore the program provided two summers of activities; in each, students took remedial classes for half the day and worked for the remainder of the day, receiving an opportunity to learn work-related skills and to earn money. The inclusion of both school-based and work-based components in theory enabled students to see how academic competencies are necessary on the job and to use the work component to explore the importance of initiative, persistence, and other work-oriented behavior. In addition, because of the concern with pregnancy as a barrier to school completion, a half-day each week was devoted to discussion of issues related to responsible sexual behavior, contraception, and other aspects of personal responsibility. Some support services (counseling and guidance, and some tutoring) were also available during the intervening school year. Because it combined both school-based instruction and work, the STEP design incorporated several elements of the school-to-work model that has emerged recently in the United States (described in chap. 7). In addition, in replicating the program in about eighty-five sites the STEP sponsors took great care to make sure that the important elements of the model were in place everywhere.

STEP was evaluated with a random-assignment approach that compared students enrolled in both the school and the work component with others enrolled in the work component only; thus the design tested the additional effects of the summer schooling component (Grossman and Sipe, 1992; Walker and Vilella-Velez, 1992). The effects on reading and math scores and on knowledge of contraception after the first summer were positive; gains during the second summer were also positive though somewhat smaller. Unfortunately, three and one-half years after enrolling in the program, STEP youths experienced the same dropout, postsecondary enrollment, employment, and teenage pregnancy rates as the control group. One widely cited conclusion from the STEP experiment is that a short-term program may improve short-term academic performance; however, a limited intervention that leaves unchanged the rest of schooling, the meager opportunities in the youth labor market, and the general environment of poor youths cannot change long-term results and fundamental behavior that results in unemployment and pregnancy.

My own observations also suggest that the implementation of STEP may have badly undermined its intentions.[14] In practice the quality of work placements was poor, jobs required almost nothing in the way of school skills, job experiences were never incorporated into the schooling component, and the classes used largely a conventional didactic, teacher-centered format and contrived materials that the majority of students—and certainly those who are considered "at risk" of school failure—find unbearable. The students we interviewed stayed in the program because they were being paid but said nothing else good about it. What students may have learned from STEP is that school is irrelevant to work, that work is usually boring, and that school never gets any better, even in special programs—not the conclusions one would want any teenager to draw. The effectiveness of well-designed programs may lie in the details of execution. As Mies van der Rohe said, "God is in the details," and here STEP was sorely lacking.

Overall, the results of the experimental programs are disheartening. Although two identified a particular effort (CET in San Jose) as having particularly strong positive effects, the programs on the average had zero or even negative effects. To be sure, the populations included in these experiments were among the most difficult to employ (two focused on young mothers with children and two on low-income youths), but the results clarify the fact that, particularly in programs for groups like young welfare mothers and youths with special problems, the modest effects achieved in JTPA and JOBS cannot be improved merely by paying somewhat closer attention to the design of programs.

Chapter 5

---•—◆—•---

The Effectiveness of
Job Training Programs:
Specific Outcomes

THE DISCUSSION in chapter 4 of the effects of job training programs leaves unanswered a number of detailed questions, particularly about the variation in outcomes that are effectively averaged in (and therefore masked by) the overall effects of job training programs. In this chapter I consider variations in the groups receiving job training, in the services provided, and in the benefits received during different periods of time after enrollment in a program. In addition, the local administration of job training programs has led to substantial differences in the performance of local programs, as revealed by the finding in chapter 4 that one program, the Center for Employment Training, is much more effective than some of its peers. The penultimate section of this chapter therefore examines the variations among local versions of programs.

The final section adds a new dimension to the discussion of the effects of job training programs: cost-benefit analysis, which adds information about costs to information about effects on employment and earnings. The logic of cost-benefit analysis involves an *efficiency* analysis that argues that programs are worth doing only if their benefits outweigh their costs. This type of analysis contrasts with those in the earlier sections, which concentrate on the *effectiveness* of programs and imply that programs are worth doing if they are effective in increasing earnings, reducing welfare payments, or decreasing unwanted behavior like crime and teenage pregnancy. Programs can be effective but inefficient; they can also be efficient but ineffective in increasing the well-being of recipients if the benefits to taxpayers outweigh the losses to recipients. Such is almost the case for Project Independence, described below.

Job Training and Specific Population Groups

An important question is whether the effects of job training vary for different population groups—for example, whether they are greater for men than for women, for adults than for youths, for whites than for black or Hispanic individuals, or for those who are the most employment-ready than for those who have multiple barriers to employment. If analysts could identify groups for whom job training programs work better than for others, programs could target resources to those groups and increase the overall effectiveness of the limited resources available for job training or provide different services to different groups.

The early evaluations of manpower projects (see table 4.1) drew no clear conclusions about which groups benefit the most from job training. However, the evaluations of Comprehensive Employment and Training Act programs found greater effects on women than on men and on adults than on youths (see, for example, table 4.2; elsewhere in Barnow, 1986; Bloom and McLaughlin, 1982). In addition, the benefits appeared to be higher for those with little labor market experience than for those with substantial experience before enrolling in a program (Bloom and Mc-Laughlin, 1982), suggesting that job training programs might benefit those with the least skills and experience, while those with more skills and experience would simply cycle in and out of employment on their own and would not be helped by job training programs.

The results of the welfare-to-work experiments in the 1980s tended to confirm the findings that the least job-ready individuals would benefit the most. Employment increases were generally greater for women on welfare, for example, and for individuals without prior employment histories (Gueron, 1987, p. 28). A more sophisticated reading of the evidence suggests a tripartite result, presented in table 5.1: participants in the programs who were the most job ready and were first-time welfare recipients (tier 1) generally did not benefit, and participants with the most serious barriers to employment, those on welfare for more than two years and those with no prior earnings (tier 3), received low and often insignificant benefits. A group in the middle, those who had spent some prior time on welfare

Table 5.1　Change in Quarterly Earnings of AFDC Applicants and Recipients in Welfare-to-Work Programs (Dollars)

	Program				
Subgroup	San Diego	Baltimore	Virginia	Arkansas	Cook County
Tier 1					
Applicants with no prior AFDC	37	121	−13	26	—
Tier 2					
Applicant returnees	158**	188***	114*	211***	—
Applicant returnees with less than $3,000 prior earnings	151**	253***	20	202**	—
Tier 3					
All recipients	—	37	69*	19	46**
Recipients with more than two years on AFDC	—	−0	110**	14	—
Recipients with no prior earnings	—	104**	70	29	12
Recipients with no prior earnings and more than two years on AFDC	—	88	94*	28	—
All AFDC recipients					
Quarterly earnings impact	118**	96***	72**	70**	19
Average control-group earnings	773	634	541	257	451

Source: Friedlander (1988), table 1.
Statistical significance: * = 10 percent; ** = 5 percent; *** = 1 percent.

and had low earnings (tier 2), appeared to gain the most (Friedlander, 1988; Gueron and Pauly, 1991, chap. 4). Such a conclusion is consistent with earlier findings that the most job-ready individuals do not benefit much from job training and with the negative results of the experimental programs that focus on the most disadvantaged (reviewed in chapter 4).

This finding supports a "triage" policy, in which job training programs would deny access both to the most job ready (in contrast to the practice of "creaming," or selecting only the individuals with the fewest barriers to employment) and to the most disadvantaged applicants, who confront the greatest barriers to employment, or—because this practice might violate political and moral considerations—would enroll the latter group in more intensive and expensive programs than are typically offered. Conventional programs would then concentrate on the group in the middle, which might expect the most substantial gains at the lowest cost.

The recent JOBS evaluations have also generated results for specific groups within the population. For the California Greater Avenues for Independence program, one set of results tended to confirm the tripartite finding of earlier experiments: recipients of welfare who were moderately disadvantaged earned more and received lower welfare benefits than did either severely disadvantaged recipients or new applicants (Riccio, Friedlander, and Freedman, 1994, table 4.6). Unfortunately, for other groups this conceptually straightforward conclusion became less clear because the effects on subgroups varied so much among the six county programs. For example, the programs classified individuals according to whether or not they needed basic education, since those who do may need remediation before they can benefit from job training, job search assistance, or any other services and therefore may be more expensive to return to employment and less effective in finding employment after any job training program. Overall, both groups benefited from GAIN, as shown by increased earnings and reduced welfare benefits. However, one of the six counties (Riverside) increased the earnings of both groups, two (Alameda and San Diego) increased the earnings of those not needing basic education but not the other group, and two (Butte and Tulare) increased the earnings of those needing basic education but not those who did not.

In addition, long-term welfare recipients benefited in three or four of the six counties, but new applicants also benefited in two of the four counties that collected such information. The programs in Riverside and San Diego benefited both those with and those without prior employment; on the other hand, the Alameda and Los Angeles programs benefited only those without prior employment and the Butte and Tulare programs benefited only those with prior employment. These results tend to cast doubt on the triage solution suggested by earlier evaluations: at least under some conditions, in some programs, the most disadvantaged individuals can benefit from welfare-to-work programs, while in other cases the principal beneficiaries are the least disadvantaged.

The evaluation of the Florida program, Project Independence, also muddied the waters somewhat.[1] As table 4.10 showed, mothers with children aged three through five benefited much less than did mothers whose children were six and over—a result consistent with the practice of creaming. Those considered job ready (in terms of their education and prior labor market experience) benefited somewhat more than did those with less education and experience. However, individuals who had been on welfare for two years or more (who were presumably less job ready) benefited much more than did those on welfare less than two years (or those who were first-time applicants). Thus the effects for specific groups provided little clear guidance for selecting individuals for the program, save for the demonstration that mothers with young children benefit less than others do.

Evaluations of Job Training Partnership Act programs using more sophisticated random-assignment methods have confirmed the greater impact of those programs for women than for men (table 4.4), though the differences were not as great as in the earlier CETA evaluation (table 4.2), and the finding of zero or even negative effects for youths confirmed the earlier conclusion that job training might be effective for adults but not for youths. (The findings of greater effects for women are consistent with findings of greater effects for the least job ready since women are likely to have less labor force experience and to have children that complicate their employment, but the effects for adults versus youths contradict this pattern.) For other subgroups, the results were generally statistically insignificant, and the most cautious conclusion is that the groups did not differ in the benefits they received from job training (Orr and others, 1994, chap. 5, exhibits 5.8, 5.9, 5.19, 5.20). However, a more serious problem is that the differences that can be detected did not fall into any real pattern. Some of the differences confirm the conclusion that the least job-ready individuals, or those with the greatest barriers to employment, benefited the most:

- Women receiving welfare benefited more than those not on welfare, and those on welfare for two years or more benefited more than those on welfare for shorter periods.

- Women who worked less than thirteen weeks in the year prior to the program benefited more than women with less work experience.

However, other results suggested that the *most* job-ready individuals benefited the most:

- Hispanic women, who were more likely to have low levels of education and not to speak English, benefited less than white or black women.

- Women with a high school diploma or general equivalency diploma benefited more than those without such a credential.

- Women who earned four dollars per hour or more in their last job benefited more than those with lower wages or no employment, as did those with a family income over six thousand dollars per year relative to those with lower income levels.

- Women with a spouse present benefited significantly, but those without a spouse present and with a child under age four, precisely the population likely to have been included in the Minority Female Single Parent Demonstration and New Chance, also benefited.

- Men receiving no welfare payments benefited more than those on welfare.

- Men who earned four dollars per hour or more in their last job benefited more than those with lower wages or no employment, as did those with a family income over six thousand dollars per year relative to those with lower income levels.

- Men with a spouse present, who are presumably more responsible or more stable than those with no spouse, benefited more than those without a spouse.[2]

For youths, differences among subgroups are even more difficult to detect because most of the results were zero (or statistically insignificant) or negative; again there is no clear pattern to any differences that exist. It is difficult to conclude much from these results about the impact of job training on different population groups, and they certainly undermine the earlier notion that job training is most beneficial for those with the greatest barriers to employment.

After a great deal of research, therefore, the degree of effectiveness of job training programs for different subgroups remains murky. Overall, women benefit more than men, and adults more than youths, for whom the results have often been zero or negative. But at least in some programs the least job-ready individuals benefit,[3] while in others the opposite is true. This finding in turn suggests that one cannot generalize any particular strategy for selecting applicants—for example, the efforts to cream, to target job training to the most disadvantaged individuals, or to apply the triage solution suggested by table 5.1.

Specific Services

Another salient question is whether certain services provided by job training programs are more effective than others. Typically, services vary not only in their nature but also in their cost and duration: classroom training (in either remedial academic skills or vocational skills) usually lasts longer and costs more than does job search assistance, which does not pretend to enhance skills, and work experience and on-the-job training can vary substantially in duration and content. The intensity of programs offered under various job training programs has ranged from half-day sessions lasting ten weeks or so, or barely more than thirty hours of instruction, to the yearlong, residential Job Corps program with its many services, costing about $15,300 per person (in 1993 dollars). To devise the most effective or, alternatively, the most cost-effective programs, policy makers must know whether certain services are ineffective and whether certain expensive services are less effective than other, more expensive ones (or the other way around).

The early evaluations (see table 4.2) were often interpreted as supporting the greater effectiveness of on-the-job training over classroom training (for example, Taggart, 1981, p. 282). Some reviews of CETA programs similarly concluded that on-the-job training was more effective than classroom training, which in turn was more effective than work experience without a training component or associated classroom instruction (Taggart, 1981, pp. 282–88). This finding was consistent with the evidence that CETA increased earnings not by increasing wage rates—or, in economists' terms, by increasing productivity—but by increasing rates of employment, which might be improved more by on-the-job training and its attention to work-related behavior than by classroom instruction and its emphasis on cognitive and vocational skills. Similarly, Barnow (1986), reviewing more studies, concluded that public service employment and on-the-job training had greater effects than did classroom training and that work experience had no effects (or even negative effects). In addition, the early evaluations of CETA concluded that longer classroom training programs were on the whole more effective than shorter programs, especially for women (Taggart, 1981, pp. 103ff.); in part, the apparently strong results from the yearlong, residential Job Corps program (see table 4.3) strengthened the case that longer, more intensive programs would be more effective.

The JTPA evaluation, using more stringent random-assignment methods, also examined the effectiveness of different kinds of services provided. Individuals were assigned to three different services: classroom training in occupational skills; on-the-job training and job search assistance, in which individuals typically enrolled in job search assistance and then sometimes found on-the-job training or unsubsidized jobs; and a category of "other" services that might include basic or remedial education, job search assistance, work experience, and miscellaneous other services. For adults, individuals with classroom training received an average of 551 hours of services costing $3,174, substantially higher than for either on-the-job training and job search assistance (averaging 222 hours at $1,427 per person) or "other" services (204 hours at $1,116 per person). For youths, "other" services (averaging 328 hours at $2,016 per person) were almost as intensive as on-the-job training and job search assistance (317 hours at $2,755), while classroom instruction was the most intensive approach (averaging 596 hours at $3,305). To put these figures in perspective, a one-year certificate program in a community college might last thirty weeks at about 25 hours per week, or 750 hours, so the most intensive of the JTPA programs involved only two-thirds of the hours of the least intensive vocational program, and the most common services were only one-third the intensity.

However, the effects of these different services were not related to their intensity.[4] As table 5.2 indicates, women benefited most from "other" services, followed by on-the-job training and job search assistance; for men, on-the-job training and job search assistance were the most effective services (though the difference is statistically insignificant). These results tend to confirm earlier findings about the superiority of on-the-job training to classroom instruction. For youths, however, the results are inconclusive because of the lack of statistical significance, though classroom training appears more beneficial (or, in reality, less harmful) than other services.

The early studies of welfare-to-work programs could not evaluate in any formal sense the effectiveness of different services because individuals were assigned to various services by nonrandom methods. The states provided different mixes of services, leading to the conclusion that different kinds of programs could all achieve the modest results found in table 4.7 (Gueron, 1987, p. 30). However, because many control group members

Table 5.2   Earnings of JTPA Enrollees, by Type of Service Used

Group	Mean Earnings of Enrollees ($)	Impact per Enrollee	
		In Dollars	As a Percent
Adult females			
Classroom training	12,008	630	5.5
OJT/JSA	17,319	2,292	15.3
Other services	14,191	3,949	38.6
Adult males			
Classroom training	19,349	1,287	7.1
OJT/JSA	23,621	2,109	9.8
Other services	20,023	941	4.9
Female youths			
Classroom training	10,279	839	8.9
OJT/JSA	14,256	−578	−3.9
Other services	$8,286	−33	−0.4
Male youth nonarrestees			
Classroom training	16,362	251	1.6
OJT/JSA	21,101	−3,012	−12.5
Other services	12,819	−438	−3.3

Source: Bloom and others (1994), exhibits 14, 15. OJT/JSA = On-the-job training and job search assistance.

in these experiments had access to education and job training programs through educational institutions and JTPA, the services provided to experimental and control groups typically differed in that the welfare-to-work programs offered brief job search assistance.

The design of the GAIN program in California reinforced this conclusion. GAIN required many participants (those with a high school diploma or a GED, or who passed a literacy test) to receive job search assistance before any other services; therefore GAIN provided predominantly short-term job search assistance, to which the generally positive effects in table 4.9 can be attributed. However, the differences among the six counties studied suggest other conclusions. In four of the six counties, large earnings gains among those in need of basic academic education indicate that remediation is an important component of job training; on the other hand, the absence of earnings gains for those needing remediation in two counties that emphasized remediation (Alameda and San Diego) indicates that basic skills instruction cannot guarantee success. Other results in Alameda also suggest that vocational training and postsecondary education can benefit participants, though two counties (Riverside and San Diego) produced large earnings increases without increasing vocational training or postsecondary education. The findings therefore suggest, as Taggart (1981) concluded from the CETA results, that effective programs can use a variety of different service strategies and that no strong evidence favors one service over another.

On the other hand, the results of the Project Independence program (see table 4.10) indicate the importance of at least some minimal level of services. The group that enrolled late in Project Independence, after a recession forced increases in caseloads without a corresponding increase in resources, did not benefit at all, presumably because they received very little from the program. (The cost per person in the "late" cohort was slightly less than nine hundred dollars, less than in almost any other job training program.) Even at its best Project Independence was not a particularly intensive program, since it provided little more than job search assistance to most clients, but the evaluation still suggests that results cannot be expected when resources dip below some critical level.

The experimental programs described in chapter 4 all involved intensive and carefully devised programs incorporating a range of services. The disappointing outcomes therefore give little support to the idea, also associated with the Job Corps, that a range of services and more intensive programs are necessary to overcome the multiple handicaps to employment of the least job-ready groups. On the other hand, the evidence for the CET in San Jose seems to support the provision of comprehensive services. This idea remains an attractive one, and I return to it in chapter 7, but neither the national JTPA evaluation nor the GAIN study nor the experimental programs of the early 1990s provide conclusive support for it.

One interpretation is that either of two very different strategies may work in job training programs. The first involves relatively inexpensive approaches. On-the-job training, which often provides little training and is little more than work experience (Kogan and others, 1989), has proved to be effective in CETA and JTPA programs; similarly, the job search assistance supported in many welfare-to-work programs appears to be modestly effective, even though it is relatively inexpensive and of short duration. Both services are designed to get individuals into employment quickly and to socialize them to the norms and values of employment, though neither enhances basic cognitive or vocational skills. The fact that job training programs have proved effective more because they enhance employment rates rather than because they increase wage rates (and presumably productivity) suggests they are effective because they move individuals into employment quickly. Whether such limited services have much effect over the long run and whether they merely substitute one group of underprepared workers for another are questions that most evaluations cannot answer. Nevertheless, in the next section I review the dismal long-run findings that are available.

The second effective strategy in job training programs is to offer more intensive services, including the kinds of remedial education supported by GAIN and various experimental programs and often combined with vocational skills training and supportive services. This intensive approach is designed to increase the competencies of individuals who are enrolled in job training programs rather than to push them into low-wage jobs and to increase their productivity and wage rates over the long run. These two strategies serve somewhat different purposes, and, more to the point, they can be linked, as I argue in chapter 7.

Finally, one service, guidance and counseling, presents a special problem. Some programs, especially intensive experimental programs like New Chance and the MFSP Demonstration, as well as the Job Corps, provide guidance and counseling, sometimes related to personal problems like drug abuse and personal relationships and sometimes related to career choices. These intensive programs often find themselves forced to provide such services, both because the individuals in them have serious personal problems that impede their learning and subsequent employment and because decisions about education and training programs—including the decision to participate or not—are unlikely to be rational and self-interested if individuals have no sense of the employment futures open to them.

In spite of their presence in job training programs, the evaluation literature contains almost no mention of guidance and counseling, save for the positive but desperately brief description of mentoring in the New Chance program (Quint, Musick, and Ladner, 1994); in addition, the evaluation of a program for teenagers on welfare, the Learning, Earning, and Parenting program, showed that programs "enhanced" with guidance and counseling increased rates of receiving high school diplomas and GEDs somewhat (Long, Wood, and Kopp, 1994). Little discussion has taken place in the job training field on what the character of guidance and counseling should be, though a related literature on the "caseworker function" (Weil,

Karls, and Associates, 1985) and some examination of different forms of "mentoring" (Mecartney, Styles, and Morrow, 1994; Morrow and Styles, 1995) exist. In contrast, at the high school level considerable discussion has focused on guidance and counseling but has resulted in little advance in practice, only partly because of budget constraints. Many providers recognize guidance and counseling as a crucial component of job training programs, although funding and consensus about what is appropriate are lacking.[5]

The Expansion or Decay of Benefits over Time

The majority of job training programs are short term, lasting perhaps fifteen to twenty weeks; and they are generally self-contained, so that individuals enrolling in them do not typically enroll in other programs to continue the process of education and job training.[6] Therefore job training programs are usually one-shot efforts to get individuals into employment rather than the beginning of a long period of education and job training (as, for example, postsecondary education can be). This characteristic raises the question of what the long-term benefits of short-term programs are. If, consistent with the human capital model, job training programs provide their clients with real skills (cognitive, behavioral, or vocational) that increase their productivity and are valued in the labor market, one would expect them to increase wage rates and earnings permanently. If the initial enhancement of skills also allows individuals to enter "careers" with subsequent on-the-job training that further increases productivity, one would expect wage rates and earnings to continue to increase over time, as happens in the age-earnings profiles associated with different levels of formal schooling. If, however, job training programs merely push individuals into the labor force without increasing their skills substantially and fail to gain them access to "careers" or positions with long-run possibilities for advancement, then the effects of such programs may be short term, and even positive short-term benefits may become essentially zero long-run benefits. Indeed, the fade-out or decay of benefits in various education programs, including STEP, has led many evaluators to conclude that *sustained* interventions are necessary to improve the life chances of low-income individuals.

Thus it is important to examine the benefits of job training programs over time to see whether any initial benefits are sustained, increase, or decay. Unfortunately, such an examination has not been easy; most evalu-

**Table 5.3   Earnings of JTPA Enrollees, by Target Group
and Follow-up Period**

Group and Period	Mean Earnings of Enrollees ($)	Impact per Enrollee	
		In Dollars	As a Percent
Adult females			
Months 1–6	2,138	170*	8.6
Months 7–18	5,794	820***	16.5
Months 19–30	6,292	847***	15.6
Total	14,224	1,837***	14.8
Adult males			
Months 1–6	3,718	204	5.8
Months 7–18	8,807	538	6.5
Months 19–30	8,996	856**	10.5
Total	21,521	1,599*	8.0
Female youths			
Months 1–6	1,564	−5	−0.3
Months 7–18	4,199	53	1.3
Months 19–30	4,744	162	3.5
Total	10,508	210	2.0
Male youth nonarrestees			
Months 1–6	2,628	61	2.4
Months 7–18	6,538	−289	−4.2
Months 19–30	7,252	−639	−8.1
Total	16,418	−868	−5.0

Source: Bloom and others (1994), exhibit 6.
Statistical significance: *** = 1 percent; ** = 5 percent; * = 10 percent.

ations last a short time, so they do not reveal the long-term effects of programs. However, a few studies shed some light.[7] Table 5.3, for example, shows the pattern of earnings for different periods over the thirty months of the JTPA evaluation (Bloom and others, 1994; summarized in table 4.4). During the first six months, earnings essentially did not increase because individuals left the labor force to enroll in the program. In the next twelve months (months 7–18), the earnings advantage for participants increased to an average of $68 per month among women and $45 among men; in the next twelve months this advantage is sustained at about $71 per month among women and men (and becomes statistically significant among men). These figures contain no evidence of a further expansion of benefits, but neither do they indicate any fade-out. (Youths, not surprisingly given the negative results in table 4.4, show no pattern of benefits at any time during the thirty months.) Similarly, the results for JOBSTART (table 4.14) suggest that the earnings of those enrolling are initially lower than those of the control group (as are hours worked) but then increase to a plateau of about $400 per year more than those in the control group, although employment rates, after increasing in year 2, seem to fade. However, the Project Independence results (table 4.10) indicate some fade-out or decay in benefits: increases in earnings and employment and decreases in welfare payments are greater in year 1 than in year 2.

The evaluations based on the longest period of time involved four welfare-to-work experiments begun during the 1980s in Virginia, Arkansas, Baltimore, and San Diego (Friedlander and Burtless, 1995). Figure 5.1 presents the effects of these programs on annual earnings and payments from Aid to Families with Dependent Children over the five-year follow-up period, as well as on welfare payments; the actual figures for employment rates and earnings are given in table 5.4. In the top panel of the figure, the dominant pattern is for earnings increases to be trivial in the first year, to increase in year 2, to remain substantial in years 3 and 4, but to fade in years 4 and 5. Similarly, welfare savings were typically trivial in year 1, increased, but faded in years 4 and 5. (Note that the period of greatest effect includes years 2 and 3, precisely the period covered by months 19–30 in the JTPA results in table 5.3.) The employment rate appears to have faded in all programs except perhaps that in Arkansas (table 5.4), and earnings to have faded except perhaps in the Baltimore program, though technical problems affected the two figures that suggest the lack of fade-out.[8] These results indicate, therefore, that the kinds of welfare-to-work programs instituted during the 1980s and largely continued in the JOBS program increase earnings and reduce welfare payments, but only in the moderate run; over the long run they leave individuals with employment rates and earnings no higher than those of welfare recipients who have not enrolled in such programs, and they do not permanently move individuals off welfare.[9]

Two possible exceptions exist to the pattern of decline over time. The only welfare-to-work program with stable benefits was the Baltimore program, in which earnings increased until year 3 and stayed about the same in year 5 (see also fig. 5.1). One possible explanation is that the Baltimore program stressed human capital development through education and

**Figure 5.1   Earnings and AFDC Payments of Welfare-to-Work
Program Participants**

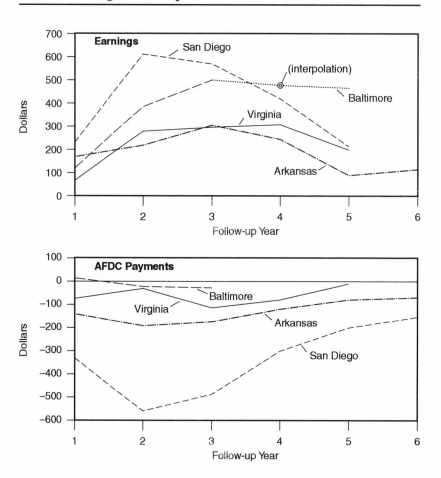

Source: Friedlander and Burtless (1995), p. 17.

training over job search intended to accelerate job finding and that the development of enhanced competencies increases earnings capacity over the longer run (Friedlander and Burtless, 1995, p. 144). In addition, the CET program in San Jose, clearly a special case, showed relatively stable increases in earnings over a five-year period, though increases in wage rates and in employment rates tended to fall (Zambrowski and Gordon, 1993).

Table 5.4 Average Employment and Earnings of Welfare-to-Work Program Participants over Five Years

Program and Year	Employment Rate (%)			Annual Earnings ($)		
	Participants	Control Group	Difference	Participants	Control Group	Difference
Virginia						
Year 1	30.4	27.9	2.6**	1,352	1,282	70
Year 2	36.7	32.7	4.0***	2,269	1,987	282**
Year 3	39.0	34.3	4.7***	2,740	2,436	304*
Year 4	41.0	39.4	1.6	3,286	2,968	318*
Year 5	41.8	40.7	1.1	3,674	3,473	201
Arkansas						
Year 1	18.5	13.5	5.0***	675	505	170**
Year 2	22.4	17.7	4.6**	1,181	956	224
Year 3	25.1	19.0	6.1***	1,440	1,122	319**
Year 4	27.5	22.4	5.1**	1,693	1,443	250
Year 5	27.7	25.2	2.5	1,890	1,800	90
Year 6	29.3	24.4	4.9**	2,108	1,995	114
Baltimore						
Year 1	30.5	27.1	3.4***	1,607	1,476	131
Year 2	38.3	34.3	4.0***	2,784	2,389	395***
Year 3	40.8	38.4	2.4*	3,497	2,991	506***
Year 4	n.a.	n.a.	n.a.	n.a.	n.a.	n.a.
Year 5	48.7	47.2	1.5	5,307	4,832	475*
San Diego						
Year 1	31.3	25.3	6.0***	1,694	1,466	228**
Year 2	35.1	27.4	7.8***	2,735	2,109	626***
Year 3	34.5	28.3	6.2***	3,205	2,623	582***
Year 4	33.6	30.5	3.1**	3,653	3,227	426*
Year 5	33.7	32.0	1.7	4,069	3,850	219

Source: Friedlander and Burtless (1995), table 4.2.
Statistical significance: *** = 1 percent; ** = 5 percent; * = 10 percent. n.a. Not available.

In general, however, these results do not suggest that benefits expand over time as a result of job training programs, as they typically do when individuals complete educational credentials like associate and baccalaureate degrees. In the first year, the benefits of job training programs are typically nonexistent or even negative because individuals withdraw from the labor force, so short-run evaluations (like that of New Chance in table 4.13) are suspect. Over the moderate run, in years 2 and 3 (and perhaps year 4 as well) the benefits increase, but after that they decay.

These findings can be interpreted either negatively, because of the lack of long-run effects of job training programs, or positively (Friedlander and Burtless, 1995). Of the four programs described in table 5.4, two saved money for governments: the reduction in welfare payments over five years ($735 in Arkansas and $1,930 in San Diego) outweighed the costs per person ($118 and $920, respectively). In all four programs the increases in earnings over five years were larger than the costs, so that from a social standpoint the benefits to all individuals—recipients plus taxpayers—outweighed the costs. In this sense these welfare-to-work programs were "worth doing," even though they did not reduce the welfare rolls or prepare individuals to leave poverty permanently.

Variation in Effectiveness among Programs

One clear implication of many evaluations is the unsurprising finding of substantial variation *among* programs. The important question, however, is whether these differences can be explained by the characteristics and quality of the programs themselves, the characteristics of individuals accepted into these programs (particularly important if some programs engage in creaming), or local economic and employment conditions. Otherwise, one would normally expect some random variation in the outcomes of programs (purely by chance some would have better outcomes than others), but such variation would not be useful to program administrators or policy makers trying to improve the quality of job training programs.

An example of variation among programs that may be purely random comes from the JTPA evaluation (summarized in table 4.4). At the end of thirty months the figures for the sixteen sites examined differed substantially: the increases in earnings varied from $2,628 to −$2,033 among women and from $5,310 to −$2,637 among men. Among youths, for whom the average effects were negative, the variation was even more marked; one program achieved statistically significant earnings increases of $3,372 among females and an impressive $9,473 among males who had not been arrested (Orr and others, 1994, exhibits 4.5, 4.16). However, partly because of small sample sizes, the differences across the sites were not statistically significant, and an analysis that tried to attribute the differences across sites to program conditions, economic conditions, and personal characteristics yielded no statistically significant results.[10]

The evaluations of welfare-to-work programs during the 1980s found that benefits were smaller in West Virginia than in other states (see table 4.7), a difference generally attributed to poor economic conditions in that state. The GAIN evaluation (table 5.5) found that the Riverside program was consistently more effective than the programs in the other five counties; indeed, the increase in earnings of nearly 50 percent for individuals in Riverside county is one of the largest effects ever found for any job training program, and the correspondingly large net benefits in Riverside suggest that well-designed programs can save taxpayers money by reducing welfare costs sufficiently (see table 5.9 below). Conversely, however, the GAIN results indicate that even a state that imposes a certain uniformity on its welfare-to-work programs can include localities (like Los Angeles and Tulare, the latter a rural county) in which programs may have no effects on earnings at all. Indeed, the variations among sites were even greater than those revealed in table 5.5: *within* counties, benefits were substantial in outlying, largely suburban offices but either insignificant or negative in inner-city offices, suggesting that the demographic composition of the enrolled group might be responsible for the differences. However, a regression-based analysis controlling for demographic characteristics did not eliminate the substantial differences among counties and among offices within counties (Riccio, Friedlander, and Freedman, 1994, table 4-7.2), and in any case some counties were successful with those not needing basic skills while others succeeded with those who were less job ready, suggesting that different counties can be successful with different groups of clients.

Nor did variations in local economic conditions—measured, for example, by unemployment rates and the growth rate of employment—explain differences; in particular, the effects of the Riverside program were remarkably consistent, even though economic conditions there varied widely during the period of the study and among local offices. Nor was there any obvious explanation of differences among counties based on the kinds of services offered. In the end, the evaluators concluded that the Riverside program succeeded because of the combination of practices

Table 5.5 Average Earnings and AFDC Payments of Single Parents in GAIN, by County

County	Earnings ($)				AFDC Payments ($)			
	Participants	Control Group	Difference	Change (%)	Participants	Control Group	Difference	Change (%)
Alameda	6,432	4,941	1,492**	30	17,593	18,375	−782*	−4
Butte	8,637	7,163	1,474	21	11,659	12,635	-976	−8
Los Angeles	4,943	4,683	260	0	17,314	18,319	−1,005***	−5
Riverside	9,448	6,335	3,113***	49	11,284	13,276	−1,983***	−15
San Diego	9,786	8,014	1,772***	22	13,283	14,419	−1,136***	−8
Tulare	7,439	7,066	374	5	15,653	15,538	114	1
All counties	7,781	6,367	1,414***	22	14,464	15,426	−961***	−6

Source: Riccio, Friedlander, and Freedman (1994), table 1.
Statistical significance: *** = 1 percent; ** = 5 percent; * = 10 percent.

there: a strong message to participants about the importance of getting into jobs early; a strong commitment to job search and job placement efforts; a mix of job search, education, and training; and a commitment to enforcing mandatory participation of all eligible welfare recipients (Riccio, Friedlander, and Freedman, 1994, chap. 8). Another observer has concluded that the high expectations of the program staff were responsible (Bardach, 1993), and still others have attributed the success to the energy and charisma of the director.

The evaluation of Project Independence also found great differences among counties, ranging from earnings increases over two years of $1,333 to earnings losses of $570 (Kemple, Friedlander, and Fellerath, 1995, table 6.13). However, these differences were neither statistically significant (that is, they may have been generated simply by chance) nor related in any obvious way to variation in labor market conditions, services available, or patterns in program participation. Such results add to the conclusion that, although differences among programs appear large, it is not yet possible to explain them by labor market conditions or by program characteristics that could be affected by policy.

The evaluations of experimental programs reviewed in chapter 4 also featured large differences among programs. Particularly striking was that two independent evaluations, one of JOBSTART and one of the MFSP Demonstration, found CET in San Jose, California, to be much more effective than the other programs. The MFSP Demonstration evaluators concluded that the success of CET was due to its practice of linking (or "integrating") job-specific skills with remedial education, its attention to job placement, and its provision of child care at the site (Burghardt and Gordon, 1990).

However, the truth is probably much more complex than this conclusion, and like that of the Riverside program, the success of CET probably results from a combination of factors.[11] First, the CET program has been in San Jose for a long time, and long-standing connections with employers facilitate its finding placements for its students.[12] Second, the program concentrates on Hispanics, and most of the instructors are both Hispanic and bilingual; the program is therefore providing bilingual education, job-skills instruction, and mentoring and acculturation to American practices for individuals who have just immigrated. Third, the site at San Jose performs real work—for example, it operates a child care center, a copying business, a cafeteria for CET members, and an auto repair shop, each associated with one of the job training programs—so that students receive work-based training and experience and classroom instruction in both job skills and remedial subjects. Fourth, the presence of social services at the site—child care and assistance with immigration issues and job placement—is clearly important. While CET provides both remediation and job-skills training and is particularly conscious of the need for English-language instruction, the two are not integrated in any important sense. They take place at different times of the day, and there is rarely any mention in one component of the program of the lessons from the other component—so the emphasis on CET as an "integrated" program seems misplaced.[13] But CET clearly has many other positive elements and offers a broad range of job-related services, and it is easy to understand why it is so much more effective than other job training programs.

The conclusion to draw from both the Riverside program and CET is that a combination of practices distinguishes particularly successful programs. I return to this finding in chapter 7.

Cost-Benefit Analyses of Job Training Programs

The results presented so far describe the outcomes of job training programs and the degree to which they improve employment rates and earnings (or other potential outcomes like arrest rates, welfare receipt, and fertility behavior). A different way of asking whether job training programs are "worth doing" is to compare the outcomes to the costs. Since the late 1970s, many job training programs have been subjected to analyses that use generally accepted methods to establish the net present value of the outcomes that could be attributed to the program—that is, the difference in outcomes between those enrolling in the program and a control group. In most cases the additional earnings of those enrolled and the reduction in welfare benefits represent the major benefits, though in some cases the value of crime prevented and drug and alcohol abuse avoided are counted among the benefits (such as in the cost-benefit analysis of the Job Corps in table 5.6). Job training also yields numerous intangible benefits, especially those associated with greater economic independence and reduced use of welfare programs, and some uncounted costs as well, particularly the opportunity costs of mothers with young children, who might otherwise be caring for them.

Typically these analyses calculate costs and benefits separately for different groups of potential beneficiaries, usually including those enrolled and the "rest of society" (or taxpayers), in order to capture the distributional

Table 5.6   Benefits and Costs per Member of Job Corps (1977 Dollars)

Component	Society	Job Corps Members	Rest of Society
Benefits			
Output produced by members	4,653	3,397	1,255
Reduced dependence on transfer programs	158	−1,357	1,515
Reduced criminal activity	2,112	−169	2,281
Reduced drug and alcohol use	30	0	30
Utilization of alternative services	390	−49.	439
Other benefits	+	+	+
Total benefits	7,343	1,823	5,520
Costs			
Program operating expenditures	1,449	−1,208	5,351
Opportunity cost of member labor	881	728	153
Unbudgeted expenditures other than member labor	46	−185	231
Total costs	5,070	−665	5,736
Net present value (benefits less costs)	2,271	2,485	−214
Benefit-cost ratio	1.45	1.82	0.96

Source: Long, Mallar, and Thornton (1981), table 6.
Note: Benefits not assigned a dollar value are shown as +.

effects of job training. That is, such programs may benefit those enrolled while taxpayers lose, or conversely the benefits to taxpayers through decreased welfare and crime costs may outweigh the costs of the programs, even though those enrolled do not earn enough to offset the loss of welfare benefits.[14] The hope of job training programs, of course, is that both taxpayers and those enrolled will enjoy benefits in excess of costs.

One of the earliest and most influential cost-benefit analyses was that of the residential Job Corps program (Long, Mallar, and Thornton, 1981), summarized in table 5.6. The results of this analysis are fairly typical of subsequent analyses: overall the net benefits to those enrolled in the Job Corps were positive. The increased earnings per person ($3,397) were high enough to offset the lost welfare income ($1,357), the opportunity costs associated with being unable to work during the program ($728), and other costs associated with being in the program. But the Job Corps was a net loss to taxpayers, since the benefits from taxes on increased earnings ($1,255), reductions in welfare benefits and administrative costs ($1,515), and reduced criminal activity ($2,281) failed to offset the very high cost of the program ($5,351 in 1977 dollars and more than $15,000 in 1995). From a social point of view, the benefits to Job Corps members plus those to taxpayers outweighed the costs; the general lesson from this analysis was that even an expensive job training program could demonstrate its worth in cost-benefit terms.

Similarly, the welfare-to-work programs developed during the 1980s were evaluated using cost-benefit analyses. Table 5.7 presents the results of a typical and particularly influential analysis, of the San Diego program, for both a work experience program and job search assistance. The results, as for the Job Corps, indicate net benefits for those enrolled in the program, as earnings increased by a small amount (for example, $461 for work experience and job search together), but net losses for taxpayers, as the costs of the program were higher than any reduction in welfare payments or increase in taxes on higher earnings. Since from a social perspective the benefits outweighed the costs, the results of this experiment were thought to confirm that welfare-to-work programs were worth undertaking and were widely cited in legislation for the JOBS program. However, the San Diego program clearly did not fulfill the fondest hopes of those hostile to welfare—that job training programs would save money for taxpayers.

In the general analysis of JTPA programs (Bloom and others, 1994), the cost-benefit results are consistent with the findings of the outcome studies. For adult women and adult men, who realized significant increases in earnings, the benefits outweighed the costs both for them and for society (table 5.8), though again taxpayers lost. But for youths, who suffered reductions in earnings during the program, the program generated net losses to participants as well as to taxpayers; losses per person were especially high ($2,904) in the case of young males. Job training programs seem to be a particularly poor investment for youths, and since these results became public numerous proposals to reduce or eliminate job training efforts for youths have surfaced.

The cost-benefit analysis of the GAIN program in California (Riccio, Friedlander, and Freedman, 1994; summarized in table 5.9) confirms that programs of varying effectiveness can generate different conclusions in cost-benefit analyses. This analysis distinguished three groups of potential beneficiaries: welfare recipients enrolled in GAIN; governments support-

Table 5.7 Estimated Benefits and Costs per AFDC Participant in the San Diego Welfare-to-Work Demonstration (Dollars)

Component	Job Search—EWEP			Job Search		
	Society	Applicants	Taxpayers	Society	Applicants	Taxpayers
Benefits						
Output produced by participants						
Value of in-program output	229	0	229	-1	0	-1
Increased output from employment	461	461	0	436	436	0
Increased tax payments	0	-85	85	0	-82	82
Reduced use of transfer programs						
Reduced AFDC payments	0	-187	187	0	-173	173
Reduced payments from other programs	0	177	-177	0	127	-127
Reduced AFDC administrative costs	14	0	14	13	0	13
Reduced administrative costs of other programs	-16	0	-16	-12	0	-12
Preference for work over welfare	+	+	+	+	+	+
Reduced use of other programs						
Reduced allowances	0	-6	6	0	-7	7
Reduced operating costs	50	0	50	45	0	45
Costs						
Program operating costs						
EPP operating costs	-366	0	-366	-383	0	-383
EWEP operating costs	-73	0	-73	0	0	0
Allowances and support services	0	22	-22	0	12	-12
Participant out-of-pocket expenses	-15	-15	0	0	0	0
Forgone personal and family activities	-	-	0	-	-	0
Net value (benefits minus costs)	280	367	-87	98	313	-215

Source: Goldman and others (1985), table 6.7.
Note: Components not assigned a dollar value are shown as a benefit (+), a cost (−), or neither (0). EWEP = Experimental Work Experience Program; EPP = Employment Preparation Program.

Table 5.8   Benefits and Costs of JTPA per Enrollee, by Target Group (Dollars)

Component	Target Group		
	Enrollees	All Others	Society
Adult females			
Earnings gain (minus OJT subsidy)	1,703	—	1,707
Training cost	56	−1,227	−1,171
Welfare benefit reduction	−235	235	—
OJT wage subsidy	154	−154	—
Net benefits	1,678	−1,146	532
Adult males			
Earnings gain (minus OJT subsidy)	1,401	—	1,401
Training cost	100	−931	−831
Welfare benefit reduction	334	−334	—
OJT wage subsidy	244	−244	—
Net benefits	2,079	−1,509	570
Female youths			
Earnings gain (minus OJT subsidy)	146	—	146
Training cost	76	−1,392	−1,316
Welfare benefit reduction	−379	379	—
OJT wage subsidy	74	−74	—
Net benefits	−83	−1,087	−1,170
Male youth nonarrestees			
Earnings gain (minus OJT subsidy)	−949	—	−949
Training cost	110	−2,065	−1,955
Welfare benefit reduction	119	−119	—
OJT wage subsidy	100	−100	—
Net benefits	−620	−2,284	−2,904

Source: Bloom and others (1994), exhibit 16. OJT = on-the-job training.

ing the costs of GAIN; and taxpayers, who also pay for GAIN through their taxes but who experience certain benefits and costs (for example, the output associated with unpaid work experience) that do not directly affect government budgets. The results indicate that both government budgets and taxpayers lost for all groups of recipients; only in the case of recipients not needing basic remedial education, which requires relatively expensive classroom training and not simply low-cost job search assistance, did the benefits outweigh costs both to recipients themselves and to taxpayers. But

Table 5.9 Benefits and Costs of GAIN, by Target Group (1993 Dollars)

	Net present value of benefits minus costs for			
Target Group	Welfare Recipients	Government Budgets	Taxpayers	Society (Taxpayers and Recipients)
All single parents	923	−833	−990	−67
Single parents not needing basic education	2,340	−622	−824	1,516
Single parents needing basic education	−117	−391	−530	−647
Heads of two-parent families	−186	−607	−652	−838
Single parents in				
Alameda	1,090	−3,054	−3,193	−2,103
Butte	1,585	54	−133	1,452
Los Angeles	−1,561	−3,442	−3,485	−5,046
Riverside	1,900	2,936	2,559	4,458
San Diego	948	767	702	1,649
Tulane	1,577	−2,261	−2,396	−819

Source: Riccio, Friedlander, and Freedman (1994), tables 7.7, 7.10.

the details for individual county programs reveal that the most effective programs, those in Riverside and San Diego, can generate savings for taxpayers as well as substantial net benefits for recipients; indeed, in Riverside the benefits to government and to taxpayers were larger than those to recipients. (And, on the contrary, the worst program, in Los Angeles County, actually made recipients worse off, as JTPA did for youths.) These results show that the hopes for the success of welfare-to-work programs lie in their ability to emulate the characteristics of the most effective programs, since on the average the GAIN program generated net losses to society.

The results for Project Independence are somewhat different than those for virtually any other job training program (Kemple, Friedlander, and Fellerath, 1995; see table 5.10). Because this program did not increase earnings by much but reduced welfare benefits, the net effects for those on welfare were actually negative. However, because it did not cost much (an average of $1,150 per person) and it did reduce welfare costs considerably (about $1,155, according to the figures in table 5.10), the program

Table 5.10   Five-Year Estimated Net Gains, Losses, and Returns per Member of Project Independence (1993 Dollars)

Component	Welfare Sample	Government Budget	Taxpayer	Society
Earnings	600	0	0	600
Fringe benefits	89	0	0	89
Tax payments				
Payroll taxes	−46	92	46	0
Income and sales taxes	23	−25	−25	0
Transfer programs				
AFDC payments	−422	422	422	0
Food stamps	−209	209	209	0
UI compensation	24	−24	−24	0
Total Medicaid	−430	430	430	0
Transfer administrative costs	0	118	118	118
Net cost of project				
Independence and non−Project Independence activities and services	0	−1,150	−1,150	−1,150
Preference for work over welfare	+	0	+	+
Forgone personal and family activities	−	0	0	−
Value of education not reflected in earnings	+	0	+	+
Net gain or loss (net present value)	−369	72	26	−343
Return to government budget per net dollar invested in Project Independence and non−Project Independence activities and services	—	1.06/$1	1.02/$1	—

Source: Kemple, Friedlander, and Fellerath (1995), table 7.5.
Note: Components not assigned a dollar value are shown as a benefit (+), a cost (−), or neither (0). UI = unemployment insurance.

**Table 5.11   Benefits and Costs of the JOBSTART Program
(1986 Dollars)**

Component	Program Participants	Taxpayers	Society
Increased earnings and fringe benefits	69	0	69
Increased tax payments			
Payroll taxes	−	+	0
Income and sales taxes	−	+	0
Reduced use of transfer programs			
AFDC payments	74	−74	0
Food stamp payments	−34	34	0
General assistance payments	28	−28	0
Payments from other public programs	−	+	0
AFDC administrative costs	0	+	+
Food stamp administrative costs	0	+	+
Reduced use of community education and training programs	0	+	+
Reduced criminal activity and income	−	+	+
JOBSTART operating costs	0	−3,863	−3,863
Compensation for program-related expenses	0	−568	−568
Additional support services	117	−117	0
Value of education not reflected in earnings	+	+	+
Preference for work over welfare	+	+	+
Forgone leisure time and activities	−	0	−
Total	254	−4,540	−4,286

Source: Cave and others (1993), table 7.9.
Note: Components not assigned a dollar value are shown as a benefit (+), a cost (−), or neither (0).

resulted in a small saving to taxpayers—quite the opposite of the results for GAIN and most other job training programs, in which recipients gained but taxpayers lost.[15] However, overall Project Independence generated losses to society since the very small gains to taxpayers did not outweigh the high losses to welfare clients.

Any positive cost-benefit results are found in analyses of job training programs with significantly positive effects on employment. If benefits are essentially zero, then a cost-benefit analysis indicates net losses to society. Table 5.11 presents the results of a cost-benefit analysis of JOBSTART, which had largely insignificant effects (table 4.14). Consistent with these findings, the net benefits to participants were very small, and the losses to taxpayers and to society as a whole were substantial.

On the whole, however, the results of cost-benefit analyses of job training programs are relatively consistent if one ignores the evidence from the least effective programs (such as JTPA for youths), the most effective programs (like Riverside's), and special cases (like Project Independence). In general, the benefits of job training programs outweigh the costs since the modest increases in earnings are larger than the modest expenditures per person. However, the benefits accrue largely to those enrolling in job training programs, and governments (and taxpayers) typically do not benefit since their costs outweigh any benefits they receive in the form of taxes on higher earnings, reduced welfare costs, and reduced costs associated with crime and other social problems. Overall, then, job training programs are "worth doing," but it is unclear whether taxpayers would support these programs if they realized that they are likely to be net losers.

Chapter 6

The Modest Effects
of Job Training:
Alternative Explanations

T HE RESULTS from nearly thirty years of evaluating job training programs are remarkably consistent—surprisingly so, given the variation in the programs supported and the differences in the methods used to evaluate them. Many job training programs lead to increased earnings, and the benefits to society generally outweigh the costs. However, the increases in earnings, moderate by almost any standards, are insufficient to lift those enrolled in such programs out of poverty. Welfare-to-work programs also increase employment and reduce the amount of welfare payments received, but they rarely allow individuals to leave welfare. Furthermore, any benefits probably fade after four or five years: job training programs do not seem to put many individuals on career trajectories with continued earnings increases, as formal schooling does.[1]

Job training programs generally seem ineffective for some groups, youths in particular (unless the program is very intensive, as the Job Corps is, though even that program's success is now in doubt), and more effective for women than for men, but otherwise it is difficult to conclude that one group benefits more than any other. Some particularly effective programs exist, such as the Center for Employment Training and the Riverside Greater Avenues for Independence. But other programs are spectacular failures, including some experimental programs with carefully considered designs, most job training programs for youths, the worst of the GAIN programs, and Project Independence as a whole, that leave those enrolled worse off than they were before enrolling. These programs violate the first maxim of intervention: "do no harm."

The modest outcomes of job training programs can result in positive assessments, indicating that the programs are worth funding on average, or in negative assessments. In my interpretation the results are very discouraging: thirty years of experimentation with job training programs have created many programs whose benefits are quite trivial for individuals in dire need of employment and economic independence and that are completely inadequate to the task of moving them out of poverty, off welfare, or into stable employment over the long run. The puzzle is why such well-intentioned efforts have been so ineffective. In this chapter I present ten possible explanations based on the results in chapters 4 and 5, direct observations of job training programs, and comparisons with education programs. Such explanations must remain speculative, since not enough evidence is available—and may never be available—on truly effective job training programs to "prove" what works. Nonetheless, such explanations help provide a basis for recommendations, the subject of chapter 7.

Small Programs, Small Effects

The first and most obvious explanation for the ineffectiveness of job training programs is simply that most are "small": they last a very short period of time, rarely more than twenty weeks, and often provide a single service—on-the-job training, classroom training, or job search assistance—rather than a variety of complementary services. Job training administrators often take pride in this aspect of their programs. They sometimes say, for example, that they offer "Chevrolet" programs, in contrast to the "Cadillac" programs of educational institutions, by which they mean that they can get to the same destination at a much lower cost; they often scorn education programs for being too "academic" and unconcerned with immediate employment.

The individuals enrolled in job training programs often have multiple problems and several barriers to employment: they often lack job-specific skills, general academic skills, and the values (including motivation, punctuality, persistence, and the ability to work with others) necessary to find and keep employment, and some have more serious problems like drug and alcohol abuse, physical handicaps, other health problems, depression and other mental health problems that may be biological rather than experiential, and pressures from abusive family members or others. Even when enrollees do not have such problems, the gap between their needs and the scope of programs is sometimes breathtaking. For example, one job training program I observed was trying to train Spanish-speaking women to be English-proficient secretaries in a fifteen-week, part-day program. Thus a disjunction exists between the profound needs of those who have not found stable employment and the small size of job training programs; it is no surprise to find trivial effects on employment.

A useful exercise is to compare the intensity of job training programs with that of education programs, measuring intensity by expenditures. The average Job Training Partnership Act program for adult men and women cost about $2,200 in 1987–89 for a twenty-week period of enrollment (Bloom and others, 1994, exhibit 2); the cost per person in the GAIN program was about $2,300 in 1993 dollars (Riccio, Friedlander, and Freedman, 1994, p. 75). (Of course, many experimental programs are much more expensive, and the cost per Job Corps member of about $15,300 in 1993 dollars is the highest of all.) In contrast, one year (approximately thirty weeks) of full-time enrollment in a community college cost an average of $6,029 in 1992-93 (*Digest of Educational Statistics, 1995*, table 328), considerably more than the limited JTPA and GAIN programs. On the other hand, graduates of a one-year certificate program increased their earnings by about 15 percent over those of high school graduates over a long period of time in the labor force (Grubb, 1995c, table 4-2), not only over four or five years. To be sure, this comparison is not especially fair to job training programs because the characteristics of JTPA and GAIN clients are quite different from those of students enrolling in community colleges. However, it indicates that the typical job training program provides fewer services at a substantially lower cost per person to individuals with less education and (often) more personal problems than typical postsecondary occupational programs do.

The Misguided Strategy of Job Training

A second possible reason for the failure of job training programs is that the basic strategy of many programs, and virtually all welfare-to-work programs, is simply the wrong one. Most programs, including the successful Riverside program, have stressed moving individuals into employment quickly through job search assistance, work experience placements, and on-the-job training that provides relatively little actual training, despite its name. The underlying assumption is that the basic problem of the unemployed is the lack of a job and that once individuals get jobs, they will remain employed. Welfare-to-work programs are particularly insistent on the value of getting any job, and the current political rhetoric in the United States about "ending welfare as we know it" concentrates on pushing welfare recipients into work. This tactic assumes that plenty of jobs are available to those who want to work and that the appropriate motivation to work—either the "stick" of reduced welfare benefits or the "carrot" of increased incentives to work—is sufficient. Much less attention has focused on the problem of enhancing the basic cognitive, vocational, and personal competencies of job trainees, except in a limited number of intensive and experimental programs.

The success of the dominant strategy of pushing individuals into employment is confirmed by the widespread finding that job training programs increase earnings by increasing the amount of employment, not the wage rates (and presumably the productivity), of individuals. But this strategy ignores the fact that the low-skilled labor market for which job training programs prepare individuals is so unstable that, without an increase in basic skills that would enable them to escape the secondary labor market, they will continue to suffer intermittent employment, low earnings, and the discouragement that leads them back to marginal employment or welfare in the long run. (This pattern is consistent with the finding in table 5.4 that benefits declined in years 4 and 5 after welfare-to-work programs.) Furthermore, the jobs that individuals leaving such programs can typically get are so dreadful (featuring repetitive, boring work, few prospects for advancement, and often harsh and demeaning supervision) that it is no wonder that individuals leave after short periods of time. Ethnographic and journalistic accounts have sometimes stressed the difficulty of *keeping* rather than *finding* jobs (Quint, Musick, and Ladner, 1994), and a current experiment is assessing the value of continuous services intended to help individuals keep the jobs they find. But whether they will do so without changing the nature of low-wage work is an open question.

The implication of this argument is that, in the interest of greater long-run effects, more attention should focus on enhancing both basic education and job skills and less on simply getting individuals into employment.[2] Indeed, the long-run evidence on the effects of welfare-to-work programs, summarized in table 5.4, tends to confirm this statement: the only program without a long-run decay in earnings was the Baltimore welfare-to-work program, which was distinguished from the others by more intensive education and training (Friedlander and Burtless, 1995, p. 144). The most powerful evidence is the contrast between the typical job training benefits, which decay over four or five years, and the age-earnings profiles associated with different levels of education, in which the benefits of education expand over time.

The Poor Quality of Job-Related Training

When they do not emphasize pushing individuals into employment, job training programs sometimes provide (as their name implies) some training in job-specific skills. This training takes place sometimes in classroom settings and sometimes in work settings or on-the-job training.[3] However, a study of on-the-job training revealed that in a large fraction of these programs (55 percent) little or no explicit training took place: employers viewed the program as a source of subsidized labor and used individuals in routine, unskilled work without providing either job-specific or general skills (Kogan and others, 1989). This approach to on-the-job "training," which occurs in a variety of job training and apprenticeship programs, is particularly likely where employers are small, marginal, and pressed for resources.[4] In many local programs, JTPA agencies seem to act as a screen to provide such employers with a steady source of relatively stable, low-cost labor and can therefore come up with jobs for JTPA trainees, but the placements offer very little training and few long-run prospects.

To my knowledge, the quality of classroom-based job-skills instruction in job training programs has never been closely examined. Here too serious problems are likely to occur. Keeping up with technological changes is difficult enough in the more sophisticated, longer-term programs offered in community colleges and technical institutes; short-term job training programs with little funding for capital outlays must find it nearly impossible. Similarly, finding instructors from industry is difficult for postsecondary educational institutions and must be even more so in local job training programs with intermittent offerings and unstable employment of instructors. Many job training programs are operated by community-based organizations, which typically pay low wages. And because such organizations are often principally involved in other activities—for example, promoting the rights of black Americans or recent immigrants or advocating on behalf of the disabled—their experience in job training and education and their connections to employers may not be strong. While the quality of job-related instruction merits further investigation, the conditions in many job training programs are not conducive to high-quality training.

The Deep Ignorance of Good Pedagogy

Educational institutions are currently engaged in a great deal of debate about the most effective pedagogies, and reformers are making a concerted effort to replace conventional, didactic methods of teaching (skills and drills) with other approaches to teaching, associated with a very different tradition of meaning making, that enable students to be active in learning, are student centered rather than teacher directed, and use a wide variety of activities and motivation in the classroom.[5] Adult education has also developed an orthodoxy of good practice that advises programs to tailor instruction to the interests and goals of adults and to use diverse instructional methods, including more active techniques. Unfortunately, none of this discussion has affected the world of job training programs, where even the existence of a debate about pedagogy is unknown. Job training programs universally use conventional pedagogical techniques based on skills and drills, in which instructors break reading, writing, and mathematical skills into a series of tiny, inherently meaningless subskills and drill endlessly.[6] The instruction is particularly bad in programs that have adopted computer-based instruction: while administrators are often quite proud of them, the existing computer programs are the worst examples of skills and drills converted to the computer screen, with even shorter reading passages, less writing, and more trivialized arithmetic examples than found in standard textbook instruction (Weisberg, 1988). Job training administrators even take pride in distinguishing themselves from educators: they say, for example, that they are "trainers" rather than "educators," and supervisors of computer-based programs describe themselves as "managers" of the program rather than as "teachers." But this pride masks their deep ignorance of pedagogical issues and results in instruction that is quite horrifying to see.[7]

Some evidence shows that conventional didactic approaches are the least effective methods for teaching many individuals, and they are likely to be particularly ineffective for the individuals in job training programs.[8] Most have not done well in many years of conventional schooling that featured conventional didactic instruction; why they should suddenly be able to learn from this approach in very short programs with bad teaching is completely unclear. The ineffectiveness of conventional approaches to teaching may be inferred from a study of remedial education in the GAIN program: the only county with an increase in test scores was San Diego, which developed an innovative program to avoid the problems in the "school-like" adult education system. As one administrator described the program's efforts, "These people had an unproductive experience in school and were not able to benefit. We wanted to avoid the perception that they were going back. We wanted to make it different and make it work for them" (Martinson and Friedlander, 1994, p. 41).

The inability of many job training programs to understand pedagogical issues is exacerbated by the problems of hiring instructors. Little research has focused on those who teach in job training programs, but the conditions in short-term and intermittent programs, often in CBOs that offer low pay, are not conducive to hiring good teachers. Typically, instructors in job training programs receive little preparation in teaching, a further indication of the scant attention given to pedagogy. In contrast, within the U.S. schooling system, preparing teachers well and paying enough to attract a stable, experienced, and dedicated teaching force are widely discussed. The fact that job training programs have typically not even raised this issue is another sign of the unimportance of teaching and another contributor to the low quality of instruction in the programs.

Poor Placement

A convention in vocational education and job training is that the labor market value of job-specific education and training is likely to be quite low if individuals are unable to find jobs for which they have been prepared. In the world of job training, some services convey general competencies—for example, remediation should enhance basic academic skills that are useful in virtually every job, and on-the-job training and work experience that foster the personal characteristics required at work should do so, too. But a good deal of job-skill and on-the-job training is job specific and may not benefit individuals much if they fail to find related employment. The relatively little analysis of the consequences of job-related versus unrelated education and training indicates that job-related vocational education has higher economic benefits than unrelated education does (Grubb, 1995a; Rumberger and Daymont, 1984).

The evidence on related placement in job training is sparse. However, one study, the Survey of Income and Program Participation (SIPP), asked individuals whether they had received different forms of job training and whether it was related to their current employment. Among those in JTPA programs, 49 percent of men and 46 percent of women reported that they used their training on their current job; for those reporting having enrolled in CETA, 42 percent of men and 46 percent of women reported that their job training was related to their job (Grubb, 1995c). And, consistent with the hypothesis that related training has a much higher economic return, men with related JTPA training earned on average 55 percent more than did those with unrelated training, and women with related training earned 42 percent more. Men with related CETA training earned 21 percent more, and women earned 6 percent more.[9]

Thus the *average* economic benefits of job training programs—the figures that show up in formal evaluations—are as low as they are partly because they average the much lower benefits (presumably near zero) of those who failed to find related employment with the more substantial benefits of those with employment related to their job training. The conclusion from the SIPP data that only a minority of individuals are in jobs related to previous job training suggests that, even with some efforts, job training programs have not done well at placement. Alternatively, if individuals are placed in related jobs with little future, then they will normally shift over time into different occupational areas with greater prospects for mobility. Under either explanation training programs' placement efforts appear only mediocre.

"One-Shot" Job Training and the Absence of Links to Other Programs

A basic characteristic of job training programs in the United States is that, since they enroll individuals with substantial barriers to employment and provide relatively limited training, they aim to place individuals in jobs with relatively low levels of skill and pay. The limited ambitions of these programs, confirmed by the finding that increases in earnings are modest and probably decay after four or five years, may be in line with their resources, but they still do not help individuals move out of poverty or off welfare. And the emphasis on quick placement into employment, which generates modest benefits in the short run, reinforces the notion that job training should be a short, one-shot event after which individuals leave the job training system.

Typically, job training programs are not linked either to other job training programs or to education programs.[10] On occasion, job training programs refer individuals to other programs (for example, they may refer those in need of remediation to adult education programs), but little effort goes toward identifying which programs might be most effective or following individuals to make sure they enroll and complete other programs (Grubb and others, 1991). Even in welfare-to-work programs, which assign caseworkers to make sure each participant can navigate the array of services offered, individuals often become "lost" when they are referred to services but never enroll, never complete the program, or fail to enroll in subsequent programs. As one GAIN administrator in California commented about individuals referred for remedial education, the lack of information about progress means that many clients "fall into the black hole of adult basic education," staying in remedial education for long periods without much progress and without caseworkers knowing where they are (Grubb and Kalman, 1994, p. 65). When individuals complete job training programs, they are usually referred to employment, not to subsequent education, and the need for most trainees to earn a living generally precludes immediate enrollment in other education or training. The consequence is that the possibilities for expanding resources to those in job training programs—for granting them access to additional training that might lead to jobs of higher skill levels and pay—are virtually nonexistent.[11] It is not surprising that the benefits of job training seem to decay over time.

Another way to view education and training is the notion—sometimes encapsulated in the overworked phrase "lifelong learning"—that a low-level job training program would only be a first step into the labor market. If job training programs were linked to one another and to education programs, then an individual could enroll in a low-level program, complete it, and enter low-skilled and low-paid employment, and then—when time and resources permit—could continue in a more advanced job training program, or a credential program in a community college, to gain access to higher-skilled and better-paying jobs. This kind of "ladder" of opportunities would therefore take an individual at any level of skill and—in a *series* of short-term programs rather than a single, one-shot program—provide access to a range of jobs with better long-run prospects.

Labor Market Explanations

A possible explanation for the mediocre effects of job training programs on employment is simply that not enough jobs exist for unskilled and semiskilled workers, so that the labor market is unable to absorb those who complete the programs.[12] For example, the failure of welfare-to-work programs in West Virginia (see table 4.7) was generally attributed to weak economic conditions. However, in other cases blaming labor markets has proved difficult. For example, variation in labor market conditions could not explain the outcomes across the six GAIN counties of California; and the analysis of JTPA after eighteen months found no significant effect of the local unemployment rate on earnings and only a minimally significant effect of urban location on outcomes for youths (but not adults) (Bloom and others, 1993, exhibit 7.12). In addition, as pointed out in chapter 3, labor market conditions have contradictory effects: although high unemployment may make job placement more difficult, it may also cause more job-ready individuals to enroll in job training programs, making placement easier than in boom times, when individuals with the greatest barriers to employment enroll in job training programs.

In general labor market explanations have not been popular among analysts of job training programs. However, labor market conditions still may explain the mediocre effects of programs. First, relatively few studies, aside from that undertaken for the JTPA evaluation, have examined labor market effects systematically, and that examination may have been marred by insufficient variation in labor market conditions.[13] Second, the weak condition of labor markets for modestly skilled work may explain the pervasively mediocre results of job training programs even if it fails to explain the cross-sectional variation in outcomes.

Finally, job training programs represent a supply-side solution to the problem of underemployment and poverty. The assumption is that, if the skills of the labor force improve or if individuals out of the labor force can be induced to enter it, then employment and earnings will improve without intervention on the demand side. The alternative tactic is to coordinate a supply-side with a demand-side policy in order to increase the demand for modestly skilled workers. Indeed, something like this tactic took place in the last years of the CETA program, when public service employment created additional jobs for CETA trainees in governmental and nonprofit CBOs. Such efforts were denounced as "un-American" since they might substitute public employment for private employment and were quickly abolished by the Reagan administration. But the notion of coordinating demand-side policy in labor markets with the more common supply-side policy remains attractive and might improve the mediocre effects of job training programs. The elements of a demand-side policy might include public service employment, disincentives to moving modestly skilled employment out of an area, and perhaps tax credits and other incentives for job creation.

Local Political Interference

Many job training programs, particularly those operated by JTPA and Job Opportunities and Basic Skills Training (which often works through JTPA programs), are highly local. A local decision-making authority, the Private Industry Council, makes important decisions about the nature of services provided and to which groups of individuals and establishes the methods for subcontracting with other groups (typically CBOs, educational institutions, and proprietary schools) that deliver the services. The local nature of these decisions is certainly appropriate because low- and middle-skilled labor markets are themselves quite local and programs must adjust themselves to local conditions. However, job training programs are also vulnerable to local political influence that sometimes directs funds to particular providers of services whether they are effective or not and makes it difficult for local programs to shift resources from ineffective providers to effective ones.

Political interference appears to take place in several different ways.[14] In some cases, providers of training services represented on the PIC direct contracts to their own organizations. In other cases, influential local politicians can effectively threaten to create trouble for a job training program if it does not support a favorite local provider. In still other cases a local job training administration, anticipating political problems, arranges to allocate resources through noncompetitive processes that contrive to award funding to particular CBOs.[15]

In many cases, political interference takes place on behalf of groups with particular racial identities—for example, a local group representing the black or the Hispanic community (or parts of a community like Haitians or Puerto Ricans). In other cases the CBOs represent women, older women trying to reenter the work force, the handicapped, or another group. Such CBOs operate simultaneously as advocates for "their" group, as sources of guidance and counseling for group members, and as providers of education and training services through public funding. In all these cases, constituents served by CBOs can exert considerable political pressure. Unfortunately, some of the worst job training programs take place in cities that have well-organized minority CBOs with political influence; the difficulty of detecting political interference is compounded by racial tensions, which make it difficult for white administrators at the local or state level to challenge the allocations of funds to ineffective black or Hispanic groups. Conversely, many of the best programs take place in rural and suburban areas that are relatively free of such political interference.[16]

The effect of local political interference on the effectiveness of job training programs is difficult to assess. In many cases, ineffective organizations are given resources because of political interference, and effectiveness suffers. However, many CBOs with political influence are extremely effective organizations, highly dedicated to the groups they serve. My hunch is that, as is generally true of private sector versus public sector programs, the CBOs include some of the best as well as some of the worst providers of job training services. The problem with local political influence is that eliminating some of the worst providers becomes difficult, and those who enroll in their programs are the ones who suffer.

The Special Problems of Youth Programs

The results of evaluating youth programs since the 1970s have been especially dismal. Many of the early CETA programs for youths had negative results (see table 4.2), and the more sophisticated JTPA evaluation also showed minimal or negative effects (tables 4.4–4.6). Several experimental programs for youth, like JOBSTART and the Summer Training and Employment Program, have proved ineffective despite careful planning and higher costs. These results are particularly discouraging because of the hope that programs aimed at youths could steer them onto paths that would be beneficial in later years.

The particularly poor results in youth programs have several explanations. One has to do with labor market conditions: many employers will not hire young people, so under the best of conditions they tend to "mill around" in the job market until they reach their early or mid-twenties.

In addition, employers will not consider individuals without a high school diploma for many moderately skilled jobs in the sub-baccalaureate labor market, effectively condemning dropouts to completely unskilled positions. Other explanations depend on the special characteristics of youth culture in the United States: its rejection of school and discipline and the premium placed on "coolness" may work against job training programs in ways that do not affect the performance of adults with more maturity and a greater sense of responsibility. Still other explanations point out that adolescents are still entangled in their families, which may be disorganized and destructive rather than supportive (Quint, Musick, and Ladner, 1994).

Unfortunately, job training programs cannot do much about these factors. However, programs as applied to young people may suffer from some systematic failings (Doolittle, no date; Granger, 1994). Programs devised for adults may not be developmentally appropriate for adolescents, and youths may especially abhor the conventional skills-and-drills pedagogy of most job training because of their recent and negative experiences with school. Because of the complex conditions of their lives, young people may need a greater variety of support services, especially guidance and counseling on such issues as drugs, alcohol, sex, and sexually transmitted diseases, that are not usually part of job training programs designed for adults. The minimal results of programs designed with a range of services, like New Chance and JOBSTART, are not especially encouraging, but most efforts to devise better youth programs still concentrate on specifying a broader array of services to cope with the complex conditions of adolescents' lives.

The Impossibility of "Second-Chance" Programs?

A final explanation for the weak effects of job training programs is that the very idea of providing "second-chance" programs may be flawed. In the United States the "first-chance" programs include the elementary-secondary education system, with its many remedial and compensatory programs, and a higher education system that virtually guarantees a place for everyone (in open-access community colleges if not in four-year colleges) and that, despite its many flaws, is more extensive, inclusive, and egalitarian than that in any other country with such a heterogeneous population. Arguably, the individuals who fail to use the educational system to increase their skills and gain access to employment are by definition those with such serious intellectual, personal, and motivational barriers to employment that no second-chance system of reasonable cost could possibly help them enter stable employment. Under this argument, the resources that currently go into job training programs should be diverted into improving first-chance programs; an alternative argument is that too much money has already been spent on preventing school failure within first-chance educational programs and that the education and training system should devote less of its resources to the bottom tenth of the population it serves, those sometimes demeaned as the "leftovers" (Taggart, 1981).[17]

But the abandonment of second-chance opportunities in job training programs and such institutions as adult education and community colleges is a distinctly un-American idea. Even in the midst of the current swing toward the political right that has spawned many proposals for dismantling important aspects of U.S. welfare and regulatory systems, almost no one calls for the dismantling of the education and training system as a whole (though little doubt remains that federal support for education and training will be curtailed). One reason is that even the most ineffective efforts at training for employment are more palatable than the alternative—allowing individuals to live at public expense without working. And the effort to build second-chance programs is an expression of the enduring American commitment to equity in some form, even if that form is not particularly effective. For these reasons the United States is unlikely to abandon its current efforts at work-related education and job training. Daunting as it may be, the appropriate task is to improve job training programs, not to abolish them.

Chapter 7

Reintegrating Education and Job Training

H OW MIGHT job training programs be improved? Drawing on the explanations for the ineffectiveness of job training programs outlined in chapter 6, one tactic might be to make each component more effective. That is, programs need to examine the quality of job training and improve it; the nature of instruction in basic skills is often very poor, and job training programs need to learn from the education system about appropriate instructional methods; and programs may need to strengthen efforts in assessment, guidance and counseling (or case management), and placement (see, for example, Dickinson, Kogan, and Means, 1994; Dickinson and others, 1993).

But this piecemeal approach, valuable though it might be in specific instances, misses the point. The real problem with existing job training programs is not that a component here or there is inadequate but that their offerings consist of a welter of different services, some job-specific training, some remedial instruction, some work experience, and some supportive services, none obviously more effective than any others and all poorly coordinated. Furthermore, individual programs of limited intensity are not linked to other opportunities, even though they are intended for a population with substantial needs. In contrast, the few effective programs—the Center for Employment Training and the Riverside Greater Avenues for Independence, for example—seem to work because they encompass a combination of mutually supporting practices. The success of these programs suggests that the most powerful approach to reforming job training is first to create more coherent systems of comprehensive employment-related services and then to worry about the quality of individual components.

Furthermore, one crucial element in improving job training programs is to connect them to other training and education opportunities rather than leave them independent, limited, "one-shot" efforts. The effects of job training programs, small as they are, tend to decay over time, while the benefits of education typically increase with further labor market experience. As it now stands, virtually the only way to get low-income individuals out of poverty or off welfare is to get them into education programs, like the certificate and associate degree programs of community colleges that have prospects for enhancing earnings.[1] The disconnection of education from job training, rooted in the creation of job training programs during the 1960s, has been counterproductive for both. Many of the reasons given in chapter 6 for the ineffectiveness of job training—including the small scale of job training efforts, ineffective pedagogy, the provision of services in small, unstable organizations, and political influences in job training—come from this divorce. And conversely, education institutions could learn much from job training programs about the importance of employment and of services like job placement.

Therefore one way to develop a more effective education and job training *system* would be to recombine them—to link job training with educational programs, using the community college (and perhaps other postsecondary institutions) as the conduit between the two to create a continuous system offering a greater variety of services for a broader range of individuals than either one now serves.[2] The trick to creating an overall education and job training system from the two currently disjointed systems is to fashion these links systematically, in "ladders" of education and training opportunities that can move individuals from their existing levels of accomplishment to higher levels at which they prepare for jobs of increasing skill, earnings, and stability.

The creation of such a coherent system would build on two other developments. One is quite general: Americans are great system builders. Throughout the nineteenth century and into the twentieth, reformers tried to develop systemic approaches to social and economic policy, creating transportation systems, a justice system, a social security system for the elderly, a comprehensive approach to imports and tariffs, and a tax system. So too in education: in the nineteenth and early twentieth centuries the United States built an education system by creating a smooth progression of public education from kindergarten through a sequence of grades, with each a prerequisite for the next, up to higher education. The result is a series of institutions, each with definitive characteristics, that are relatively well articulated; the requirements for progression through the system are well known and so regularized that many observers speak of the "pipeline" of education. No such system building has occurred yet in job training programs, which are too new, too variable, and too uncoordinated to have any of the stable attributes of a system. But creating coherent linkages between job training and education would advance the process of developing a more coherent system with a role both for short-term job training and for longer-term education programs with greater payoffs.

The other reason for linking education and job training in more coherent systems stems from current debates in the federal government. The current round of interest in consolidation—combining various education and training programs in large block grants allocated to states—comes in part from the perception that there are too many education and job training programs, that they are too uncoordinated, and that they contain too many possibilities for waste, overlap, and duplication. Consolidating federal programs and giving states the responsibility for running them does not resolve any of these problems; it merely hands them to states to solve (or fail to solve). But it does provide an opportunity for states to act, because whatever final form the consolidation of federal programs takes will surely loosen federal constraints and give states greater powers to combine federal with state funding as they see fit. Whether to create coherent state systems or, conversely, to continue the current hodgepodge of relatively ineffective programs is a choice that *states* will make.

Past rounds of block grants also provide some guidance on what is likely to happen under consolidation. In the block grants enacted during the Reagan administration, for example, the programs that fared best were those with statewide application and a history of state as well as federal funding; that is, states tended to shift their funding away from programs that had been totally federally funded—those, like many job training programs, that states see as not being "theirs"—to those with a historically greater state role. And they tended to shift from programs emphasizing populations with special needs, like the poor or the handicapped, to programs for which more citizens are eligible (Peterson and others, 1986, chap. 1). These past developments suggest that the consolidation of education and training programs is likely to lead over time to a shift away from special-purpose job training programs toward the broad education programs that states have always funded.[3] One implication is that short-term job training programs and programs targeted to the poor or the most disadvantaged are most likely to survive if they can become part of a larger system of education and training opportunities that states can call their own.

Implementing the School-to-Work Model

Fortunately, an existing model in the United States can serve as the basis for reforming job training, though it has not yet been implemented. The School-to-Work Opportunities Act (STWOA), passed in May 1994, is intended to apply to secondary and postsecondary education programs, but the vision it presents could guide job training programs as well. The STWOA can be interpreted as specifying five elements for successful programs:

1. *Academic instruction.* In many federal programs like those under the Job Training Partnership Act and Job Opportunities and Basic Skills Training, academic components are either remedial education or English as a second language.

2. *Vocational skills training integrated with academic (or remedial) instruction.* Integration does not imply (as it does in job training) that individuals receive both kinds of instruction at different times of day; it is a much more complex practice in which academic and occupational content are combined within a single class, sometimes with the collaboration of two different instructors (Grubb, 1995a).

3. *Work-based education coordinated with school-based instruction through "connecting activities" to provide a different kind of learning* (like the learning CET provides).

4. *The connection of every program to the next in a hierarchy of education and training opportunities.* In the STWOA, high school programs are explicitly linked to postsecondary opportunities. The analogy in job training programs is that every program would be connected to other

programs providing a higher level of skill training and access to enhanced employment opportunities.

5. *Applied teaching methods and team-teaching strategies.* By implication, all school- and work-based instruction should develop pedagogies that are contextualized, student centered, active (or constructivist), and project or activity based; they would adhere to the standards of good practice developed for adult education rather than ignoring pedagogical issues, as job training programs currently do.

Most federal job training programs now violate this vision. For example, adult remedial programs are usually freestanding entities unconnected to either vocational skills training, work-based instruction, or higher-level programs; they usually use the worst kinds of didactic instruction, often because they are driven by pressure to teach to the general equivalency diploma test (Grubb and Kalman, 1994). JTPA programs often fund on-the-job training that is intended to be a form of work-based learning, but learning on the job is often insubstantial because individuals are being used as low-cost unskilled labor (Kogan and others, 1989), and it is usually unconnected to remediation or vocational skills training. JTPA and welfare-to-work programs support occupational skill training, but these efforts are usually short term. At best they provide limited training for repetitive entry-level work, like so-called electronics programs preparing individuals for work as assemblers in high-technology factories or so-called computer programs preparing clients to be data entry clerks with spreadsheet applications, and they are unconnected to any further training or education opportunities, including certificate and associate programs. Furthermore, these job training efforts are often disconnected from the remedial instruction that many clients need, as well as from other support services.

In other cases clients receive job search assistance without either remediation, vocational skills training, or work-based learning—a particularly inappropriate program for individuals who lack both education and labor market experience. And the referral mechanisms that might lead individuals from successful completion of one program into a higher-level program or from one service (like remediation) to another (like occupational skills training) are rarely in place. While individuals can create longer programs by moving from job training into two-year colleges, for example, doing so requires the individual to take the initiative to negotiate the movement from one institution to another and from one set of eligibility requirements to another.

Thus the pieces of more coherent programs are in place, but they are currently disconnected. My vision of job training programs would integrate the resources currently available in different federal programs: for example, the remediation currently funded by the Adult Education Act, the Adult Literacy Act, JTPA, and JOBS; the vocational skills training supported by federal and state funds for vocational education, JTPA, and (sometimes) JOBS; the on-the-job training and work-based experience now funded by JOBS and potentially the STWOA; the support services funded by JTPA and JOBS; and the income maintenance available to welfare recipients in JOBS and to students through Pell grants.[4]

Developing a more coherent and integrated program of education and job training is an enormous task, and here I can only outline the necessary elements. However, if program planners keep the central vision that emerges from the STWOA in mind, then they can develop many of the elements necessary for successfully realizing it over time. The most crucial elements are the linking of programs in vertical ladders and integrating instruction and services.

Linking Programs in Vertical Ladders

A coherent system requires all programs to be linked into a series of sequential education and training-related activities that individuals can use to progress from relatively low levels of skill (and relatively unskilled and poorly paid work) to higher levels of skill and (presumably) more demanding, better-paid, and more stable occupations.[5] Figure 7.1 illustrates this concept: individuals with no occupational skills and little experience could enter short-term job training programs, the kind now provided by JTPA and welfare-to-work programs, that would provide fifteen to thirty weeks of preparation for the most modestly skilled entry-level jobs. Then individuals could *either* leave to seek employment with the help of appropriate placement services *or* enter a subsequent job training program, presumably a certificate program leading to more skilled jobs.[6] Some individuals—those without other resources, who need to support themselves immediately—would then go into employment but would be able to reenter the system late, when the conditions of their lives permit, and continue up the ladder of opportunities. The linkages among programs would be occupation specific; for example, a community-based organization or

Figure 7.1   A Unified Education and Training System

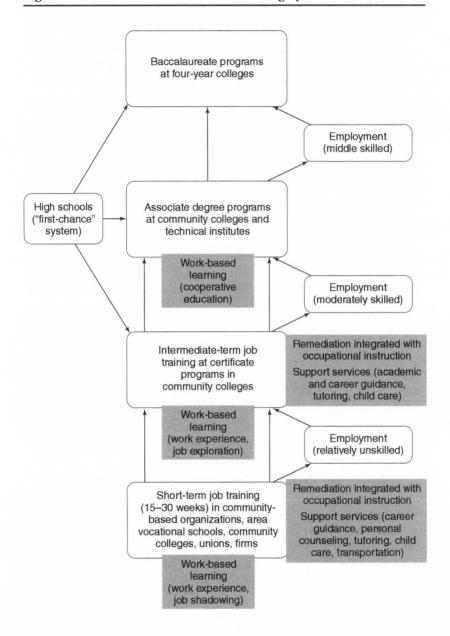

a vocational school could offer a fifteen-week job training program in electronics that leads to entry-level and relatively unskilled assembly-line employment; then, after working a while, an individual could continue in a certificate program in electronics, probably in a community college.

In turn, certificate programs would prepare individuals for employment *or* for subsequent continuation in an associate degree program, depending once again on the life circumstances of the students. For their part, associate degree programs are usually often connected to baccalaureate-level programs through the articulation agreements and transfer centers that are part of many community colleges. In this vision, institutions outside of education—CBOs, unions, and firms—as well as area vocational schools and two-year colleges could provide the lower levels of job training, but most certificate- and associate-level occupational instruction would take place in educational institutions, particularly two-year colleges. In this way two-year colleges would become the point of connection between what is now the job training system and the educational system.

One element in creating such a ladder is that every job training program in a community would be required to specify the programs to which it leads and the lower-level programs that "feed" into the program. This information would tell students the appropriate sequence of programs. In addition, the process of developing agreements among different providers would require collaboration in the design and delivery of education and training, not merely cooperation in the sense of providing information to one another. To collaborate, individual providers must view themselves as parts of a system (*noncompeting* parts, a role that might eliminate some of the turf battles that now exist) and view their mission as preparing individuals both for employment at certain levels and for continuation in the education and training system later.

In addition, the creation of vertical ladders would require the kinds of articulation mechanisms that now exist between some community colleges and four-year colleges. These mechanisms, which are intended to smooth the transition from one institution to another, typically involve the provision of information to students about subsequent requirements; agreements about the appropriate level and content of each program, including questions about courses that count for credit at the higher level; and help with the process of application. The most aggressive systems would also have mechanisms to track individuals over time in order to make sure that they do not become lost in the system and that they have access to the information they need to continue making progress. Such tracking mechanisms are similar to the caseworker function in welfare programs and to the student-tracking system devised by some colleges to provide counseling and guidance to students who fall behind their stated career goals (Palmer, 1990; Roueche and Baker, 1987, chap. 3).

A system of credentials would make the functioning of this vertical system easier. That is, if vocational education and job training programs are vertically sequenced, then it is necessary to know that an individual has mastered certain competencies before progressing to more advanced education. Existing education credentials could serve this purpose, as long as higher levels of the system accepted lower credentials as evidence of competence. Alternatively, occupation-specific skill standards created with the participation of employers, which have been attracting increasing attention, could serve as credentials.[7] However, the process of putting together a system of credentials is complex and involves many pitfalls (such as relying on standard multiple-choice tests that in turn often lead to "skills-and-drills" teaching methods), and the benefits of credentials need to be weighed against the inevitable costs.

There are several reasons for emphasizing vertical integration and the creation of education and training ladders in place of conventional forms of horizontal coordination:

- The individuals within the education and training system who are in the greatest need require a number of different services: basic language skills and other competencies; job-specific skills; personal attributes like motivation, discipline, and persistence; help in conquering drug and alcohol dependencies or mental health problems; and decision-making skills, making it difficult for them to negotiate programs on their own and requiring a counselor or caseworker. They need so many services that it is impossible to think about integrating them into the economic mainstream except in small steps and with support (via welfare, training subsidies, or unskilled work) in the interim.

- Many who need education and training must work while they are enrolled in programs. This is true almost by definition for those seeking retraining, upgrade training, and second-chance training, but it is also true for a number of those seeking initial entry into the labor force. They cannot afford to stop working for one to four years to accumulate a credential; they need instead to accumulate small amounts of education and training, work a while, and return to school (probably part time) to improve their skills further.

- Even when communities provide a range of services, the pathways through them are unclear, particularly to those who are unsophisticated about finding and using programs. Furthermore, eligibility standards are inconsistent, assessment procedures are varied, and the content of programs is uncoordinated, so in practice the range of education and services provided is not a smooth continuum.

- The labor market has certain barriers that can be overcome only through specific education credentials. The market for middle-skilled occupations is almost completely closed to individuals without high school diplomas; therefore relatively unskilled individuals (such as high school dropouts in JTPA or JOBS programs) have a chance at entry-level jobs in the middle-skilled labor market only after they get their diplomas. With experience, ability, and motivation they can advance, but some occupations may require subsequent education (for example, from community colleges or technical institutes in computer applications, specific business procedures, computer-assisted design, or specific electronics training) in order to gain entry. Many jobs—management, accounting, computer programming, frequently health care, and most professional positions with real opportunities for advancement—require a baccalaureate degree. That is, the lack of a high school diploma, of certain forms of sub-baccalaureate education, or of the baccalaureate itself can block advancement sequentially so that individuals who want to advance must go back into the education and training system to obtain further skills. This is particularly true in fields (like health care) that have codified competencies through occupational licensing; if the United States moves toward skill standards, the need for formal credentials will become routine in other occupations as well.

- Existing programs are hierarchically arranged anyway—one reason for the lack of much duplication among programs. Individuals on Aid to Families with Dependent Children are typically less well prepared and experienced than those in JTPA programs, who in turn are less well prepared than the typical community college student. In job-skills training, area vocational schools and JTPA programs provide shorter and less sophisticated programs than community colleges do. In the literacy/remediation world, community-based volunteer programs take in those who are completely nonliterate, adult education programs typically start at the fourth or fifth grade-level equivalent and lead to a GED, and community college programs usually start at a higher level and aim to prepare individuals for college-level English courses. As long as such hierarchies exist in programs, it makes sense to take advantage of them.

• Currently few mechanisms exist to uncover low quality in the system. If programs are linked vertically, a receiving program that finds preparation in the sending program to be inadequate has a new incentive for blowing the whistle on the ineffective program.

Linking the existing systems of vocational education and job training offers many advantages. The primary advantage is not that linkage would eliminate waste and duplication, since there is very little of that; instead, a unified system would be more effective, particularly for the individuals who find themselves in short-term job training programs with small and short-lived payoffs.

Integrating Support Services

In the world of job training programs, the worst-off participants suffer from multiple barriers to employment—a lack of not only basic academic capacities and job-specific skills but also the personal attributes necessary for sustained employment. They may have problems with drugs and alcohol or manifestations of mental illness; many, especially single mothers on welfare, have small children that complicate their lives and their efforts to become independent; some are saddled with families and communities that undermine their resolve and independence; and they face the same uncertainties that community college students face: how to progress in a complex, rapidly changing, and often forbidding world. These other barriers are extremely varied, but they are linked by the fact that the conventional offerings of education and job training—classroom instruction, work-based learning, job search assistance, and help with job placement—cannot overcome them.

Recognizing the multiple barriers that some individuals face, some job training programs have provided support services in addition to education and training. One of the first was the Job Corps, which offered a variety of social services in a residential setting—that is, away from the presumptively harmful families and communities from which participants came. Several other experimental programs have similarly focused on particular groups with multiple problems; for example, the Minority Female Single

Parent Demonstration provided an extensive array of services like child care, counseling, guidance in managing daily problems, and help in finding jobs after the program. Similarly, the New Chance program, also aimed at young mothers (most high school dropouts), offered remedial education, preparation for the GED, career exploration, instruction in job-finding skills, health education, family planning, and life skills; in a second phase, more employment-focused services included job training, work experience, and job placement assistance. The program also provided child care and some services to children, including health care. Finally, some of the most effective programs in the entire job training system, particularly CET and the Riverside (California) welfare-to-work program, seem to be effective because they provide a variety of services and help individuals in several distinct ways.

The strategy of providing support services is not confined to job training. In K–12 education, the provision of comprehensive services in schools—or at school sites—has been a popular idea at least since the turn of the century and has been revived in the early 1990s as the students coming to school are more likely to be poor and to need health care, food, counseling, housing, interventions with their parents, or even protective services (Kagan and others, 1995; Lewis and others, 1995). In community colleges, the provision of counseling, tutoring, and child care services has become common, as has the expansion of remedial education; many community colleges also offer special services to minority students to improve their progress through the institution. Some states have set up special centers for support services. In North Carolina, for example, such centers help the institutions accommodate JTPA and welfare clients as well as students not receiving special aid. Four-year colleges also provide an extensive array of such services even though their students are less likely to be poor or to lack parental support. Like second-chance programs themselves, the efforts to provide more comprehensive social services represent one of the most generous impulses in American policy, one that compensates for the inadequacies of many families and communities.[8]

Unfortunately, very little is known about what contributes to the effectiveness of support services.[9] The services themselves vary widely from program to program. In community colleges, where resources are quite limited, counselors have very little time to spend per student and appear to be dispensers of information rather than developers of active programs. In job training programs caseworkers are generally considered important to follow students through programs and guide and counsel students, but aside from a few experimental programs like New Chance, very few resources seem to exist in this area. Perhaps as a result, students' views of support services are quite diverse. Students often find remedial education "irrelevant," and dropout rates are high; the relationship between such forms of schooling, usually taught as decontextualized skills and drills, and their goals of improving one's prospects is too tenuous. Similarly, community college students are often dismissive of counseling and guidance; in a kind of triage, both students who are the least certain about their employment options and those who are the most certain do not use counseling and guidance (Grubb, 1996, chap. 2). However, the New Chance program made a strenuous effort to develop community-based mentors in order to help women with various aspects of child rearing, pregnancy prevention, drug and alcohol abuse, and abusive family relationships, and the participants generally reacted positively to these services; whether the services were enough to enhance their success is unclear.[10] A reasonable conclusion is that students and clients are more likely to accept intensive services offered with considerable thought about how recipients will view them, that such services are likely to make some difference, but that most programs fail to provide enough services or services of the right kind.

There is no dearth of recommendations about how to make support services more effective. But many of these repeat bromides are not particularly helpful in thinking about how best to provide supportive services. They say, for example, that services must be increased, must be provided by individuals who are "sympathetic" and "supportive" of their students and clients, or should be appropriate to the problems at hand, but the recommendations do not include a diagnosis of the problems with existing support services. However, the examples of remediation and counseling and the apparent success of services in New Chance provide a few clues. In general, remedial education has taken place in classes that are divorced from regular academic and occupational classes and has used the skills-and-drills approach, which is particularly inappropriate for older students who have already completed many years of conventional schooling. Similarly, guidance and counseling are often provided independently of other program elements by counselors who are unfamiliar with the rest of the program and usually poorly prepared to provide career-oriented counseling; indeed, complaints about counselors' ignorance of local labor market conditions and occupational offerings are common in both high schools and community colleges. Furthermore, the dominant approach to counseling appears to be the "information dump," in which individuals receive masses of information about the nature of jobs, the personal and educational prerequisites for jobs, and statistics describing labor market conditions, whether or not they can absorb this information or use it in their own decisions.[11] Similarly, education related to personal skills—for example, education about spending and saving, personal relationships, sex and contraception, and drug and alcohol abuse—very often takes the form of didactic instruction in freestanding classes unrelated to the other activities of an individual's life.

This failure of the usual recommendations to improve support services suggests that the early stages of the education and training system illustrated in figure 7.1 should incorporate a different approach. In particular, four principles ought to guide such services:

1. *Integrate support services with the other elements of a program, rather than provide them in freestanding classes or by individuals with little connection to other elements of the program.* The integrated provision of remediation (described in Grubb, 1996, chap. 6) illustrates one model; another is the inclusion of career education and career exploration around work placements, as in the Co-op Seminar of LaGuardia Community College (Grubb and Badway, 1995).

2. *Avoid didactic approaches and "information dumps," which are unlikely to be effective.* Instead, providers should consider the ability (or inability) of students to interpret or act on such information. Those who lack the ability to plan or to make decisions, for example, who are unable to consider the future consequences of present actions, or who do not understand the complex web of obligations underlying most employment are unlikely to be able to make good use of information about employment alternatives.

3. *Make support services as experience based as possible rather than independent of any specific context requiring various competencies.* Indeed, the value of incorporating various kinds of work-based learning in programs, as the STWOA recommends, is that students will have another vantage point from which to view the world that will help them understand in a more direct way the role of formal schooling and the competencies one needs at work.

4. *Make support services continuous and developmental.* That is, just as the occupational and academic skills training depicted in figure 7.1

becomes increasingly sophisticated as one moves from initial, shorter programs of the current job training system to the longer and more complex associate degree programs, any necessary support services should provide competencies and information of increasing levels of sophistication.

The details of applying such principles to efforts to provide counseling, tutoring, and instruction in personal skills are myriad and cannot be adequately developed here. In fact, the details of operation cannot be determined a priori at all, since they depend on a specific program, a particular work context, and a group of students with known backgrounds and individualized needs. What remains important is that the programs of a unified education and training system treat support services in the same integrated and developmental way that they treat occupational and academic competencies.

Implementing a Coherent System

The most important aspect of articulating a vertical system is to make sure that it provides a constant vision of how to reform existing programs. The details of these reforms are unfortunately overwhelming, and many must be worked out at the local level. Even without getting into the nuts and bolts of such changes, such a system requires five distinct changes in state policy:

1. *Designate a state agency or council to oversee its development* (for example, the Human Resource Agency permitted by the 1992 JTPA amendments). Such an agency clearly needs sufficient power to improve vertical coordination, oversee the development of improved information, and the like. What is critical for the success of such an agency, however, is that it include all relevant participants, be unbiased about the existing range of programs, and be motivated by a clear vision of a vertical ladder of programs. If the council is viewed as partisan (if, for example, it is simply the existing State Job Training Coordinating Council with a bias toward JTPA and short-term job training or the State Council on Vocational Education with its bias toward vocational programs), then it will fail to pull together all relevant groups.

2. *Designate a local or regional council to oversee its development at the local level.* The council would improve vertical articulation, oversee the local implementation of information and tracking systems, improve information available to prospective students or clients, improve the quality of local programs, and take responsibility for other interstitial and interprogram problems that arise, including the identification of "holes" in the local system for which required programs are unavailable. Like the state-level council, this group must be viewed as impartial among education and training programs; for that reason, basing it on local private industry councils, with their bias toward short-term training, or the Employment Service, with its poor reputation among employers, would be inappropriate. At the same time, the local council must be a creature of the state and an arm of state policy rather than a creature of local politics. If the local political manipulations that have hamstrung so many JTPA programs are replicated in these local councils, they will again fail to improve the existing system.

3. *Create incentives for vertical coordination and disincentives for programs to maintain their independence from others.* State governments have several incentives at their disposal: (a) the bully pulpit of the governor's office and of state agencies (including the state council); (b) various federal funds that can be allocated to provide incentives for vertical coordination;[12] (c) state regulation of local programs, which ought to require, for example, that programs referring their students or clients develop guidelines for doing so, refer individuals only to programs known to be of sufficient quality, and monitor the progress of individuals referred elsewhere; (d) state funding for community colleges, area vocational schools, and job training and welfare-to-work programs, which can be made contingent on vertical integration; and (e) performance mechanisms, including those required by federal legislation in JTPA, vocational education, GAIN, and adult education, to use as the basis of student-tracking mechanisms and to include measures of continuation in other programs.

4. *Establish information systems.* Such systems would track individuals through the system so they do not become lost, provide good information on the effectiveness of existing programs, and provide information to prospective students or clients about the effectiveness of

different programs so that they can make rational decisions about which to enter.

5. *Abolish programs that are inconsistent with the central vision and create institutions necessary for the vertical system (like the local or regional councils mentioned above).* For example, the adult basic education system in most states is extraordinarily weak and violates the notion that remediation should be integrated with job training. It should therefore be abolished and its responsibilities transferred to community colleges, which provide remediation of their own, often in more creative ways. Because of lax regulation, there are many ineffective proprietary schools that should be closed, and the quality of area vocational schools is so variable that some of their short-term job training responsibilities should probably be transferred to community colleges. To some extent, a greater emphasis within each program area on outcomes and effects in place of enrollments will mean that some programs decline while others expand. However, closing ineffective programs has always been difficult because they develop political constituencies; doing so will require a coherent state policy and state power to back it up.

A number of other issues will need to be resolved. The makeup and the responsibilities of the state and local councils are difficult political issues; states must clarify how regional or local councils will work where previous efforts have failed; the details of vertical integration are mind-numbingly complex; the political and turf battles that must be fought to establish this vision are daunting; and such a system will continue to generate new problems, for example by identifying areas of unmet needs and difficult issues of quality. However, a vision of vertical integration is more appropriate than the current system both to the existing structure of programs and to the needs of many individuals in their efforts to make their way into stable employment.

As mentioned in chapter 1, the trajectory of education and job training since the 1960s has been one of increasing variety and complexity. To some extent the developments have been beneficial: for example, institutions like the community college, which allow greater access to postsecondary education, have expanded, and training programs for the unemployed and welfare recipients are now available where none existed before.

But the conscious separation of job training from education, present at the inception of these developments, has undermined the quality of programs even as it has justified the continued proliferation of different types of programs. The conventional response to proliferation—the enactment of block grants that swallow myriad smaller programs, first in CETA and in the proposed consolidation legislation considered by Congress in the mid-1990s—has simplified the administration of the system but has failed either to bring education and job training together or to make job training noticeably more effective. The development of a single system that would reintegrate education and job training in a carefully developed progression of programs would end the fragmentation characteristic of this history and thereby develop programs more effective than those that now exist.

Chapter Notes

Chapter 1

1. CBOs are private organizations, incorporated under state laws, that provide many different social and educational services. Some of them are identified with groups of individuals. For example, a CBO might represent the black community, Hispanic migrant workers, the disabled, or older women returning to the labor force; some CBOs offer particular services, like child care or homemaker services for the elderly. In general, there is minimal government regulation of CBOs, and their quality varies greatly. For a much more positive view of CBOs than mine, see Harrison, Weiss, and Gant (1994).

2. One issue is whether any training is involved in on-the-job training or whether it is the same as short-term work experience; see the discussion in chapter 5. For evidence that much on-the-job "training" does not provide training, see Kogan and others (1989).

3. This study is not a formal meta-analysis, which would require a statistical analysis of outcome results, suitably standardized, from a large number of studies. A formal meta-analysis has been carried out by Fischer and Cordray (1995) (see also Fischer, 1995). However, as in most meta-analyses, the summarization of evidence in those works makes it difficult to understand what particular studies of which programs have contributed to the overall outcomes. Instead, I present results from specific evaluations in a series of tables illustrating the basic findings.

4. See also the similar conclusions in LaLonde (1995).

Chapter 2

1. On the history of manpower policy, see National Academy of Sciences (1975).

2. For program years 1988 and 1989, for example, the standards for adults included the percent of participants placed in jobs (with 68 percent the minimum standard), the average hourly wage at job placement ($4.95), the average cost of placement ($4,500), the percent of welfare recipients placed (56 percent), the percent of participants employed at a thirteen-week follow-up (50 percent), the number of weeks worked at follow-up (eight), and weekly earnings at follow-up ($177). The standards for youths included

123

a positive termination rate, cost per positive termination, entered employment rate, and employability enhancement rate.

3. Many other forms of aid to low-income families also constitute welfare, including food stamps, housing subsidies, child care, and other social services, and many other programs for individuals with low earnings should be considered welfare, including Social Security for the elderly. However, the political concern about welfare and efforts to reduce welfare costs almost always concentrate on AFDC first and foremost.

4. AFDC was extended to two-parent families in 1967 because of the belief that confining welfare to mothers with young children would cause some fathers to abandon their families.

5. These figures refer to participation in WIN demonstration programs (U.S. General Accounting Office, 1987).

6. Applying the term *workfare* to the experimental welfare programs of the 1980s is somewhat misleading because few of them included CWEPs or the mandatory elements that were historically part of workfare—for example, the threat that welfare recipients would lose their grants if they failed to comply with work requirements. Enrollments in these new programs were kept relatively low, partly for reasons of cost, so they emphasized voluntary rather than coerced participation.

7. Current efforts to "reform" welfare (AFDC) may eliminate the matching requirements. The likely consequence is that funding for both welfare and welfare-related training will decrease dramatically.

8. In a departure from past welfare policy, JOBS also allows families in which both parents are present in the home and the primary wage earner is unemployed to qualify for benefits and services, and it requires that one parent participate in training. However, as in WIN, funding limits mean that JOBS has not functioned as an enforceable mandate. The federal government required states to enroll 7 percent of their total welfare caseload in JOBS in 1990 and to enroll 20 percent by 1995.

9. See also the massive review of federal programs compiled by the National Commission for Employment Policy (1995).

10. Although about one-quarter of student aid goes to proprietary schools, most of the remainder goes to students in four-year colleges and universities, not to students in occupation-specific programs in public community colleges and technical institutes. Student aid therefore provides only limited support for job training.

11. See also the distinction made by Gueron and Pauly (1991) between "broad coverage" programs, which include all the elements of a complete job training program and are designed to reach a broad range of individuals (and in which welfare recipients must participate), and "selective-voluntary" programs, in which program administrators can select who can enroll or individuals can opt to participate or not. The experimental programs examined in chapter 4 are examples of selective-voluntary programs.

12. Many states provide funding per student for community colleges and technical institutes. If a JTPA or JOBS program sends an individual to a community college, state aid to the college—not JTPA or JOBS funds—pays most of the costs, making this kind of referral cheaper than paying the full costs of the program in a CBO. This cost shifting leads to individuals being funded from several public sources simultaneously: an individual in a community college could receive subsidy through state aid to the college, federal grants and loans through student aid, and subsidy under JTPA or JOBS. See Grubb and McDonnell (1991, 1996).

Chapter 3

1. CETA generated a data set, the Continuous Longitudinal Manpower Survey (CLMS), that followed several waves of CETA clients and contained information about control groups. The CLMS was used for many of the evaluations; for a survey, see Barnow (1986).

2. There has been a long-running debate over experimental versus nonexperimental methods. The early literature showed that nonexperimental methods were subject to various errors; see, for example, Ashenfelter (1978), Ashenfelter and Card (1985), and Fraker and Maynard (1987). Recently Heckman (1993) has argued that experimental methods are flawed and that newer forms of quasi-experimental evaluation may be just as accurate; see also Burtless (1995) and Heckman and Smith (1995). However, experimental methods remain the dominant form of evaluation in job training and welfare-related programs, though they have rarely been used to evaluate education programs.

3. Differences between experimental and control groups can be due to sampling error. Therefore most evaluations use regression methods to control for the effects of personal characteristics that may vary between experimental and control groups, but with the knowledge that variables describing program participation are uncorrelated with background variables or unmeasured characteristics like motivation.

4. For a more technical critique of randomized experiments, arguing for the usefulness of recent nonexperimental methods, see Heckman and Smith (1993).

5. A contrary argument could be that assignees who do not enroll find a job in the interim and are therefore more job ready and motivated. However, if this were true, then the benefit per assignee would be higher than the benefit per enrollee, contrary to the evidence.

6. This is likely to happen if the demand for labor is relatively price inelastic, in which case any shift outward in the supply function for labor will increase employment only slightly and reduce wages considerably.

Chapter 4

1. As mentioned, this book does not contain a formal meta-evaluation; for a meta-evaluation, see Fischer (1995) and Fischer and Cordray (1996). See also the recent review of education and job training programs in U.S. Department of Labor (1995) and LaLonde's (1995) brief review article.

2. This study still presents a problem of external validity despite the sophistication of the experimental designs: the sixteen programs were volunteers, and though they did not differ in any obvious way from JTPA programs as a whole, they still may have been more effective than randomly selected programs would be.

3. These results indicate the problems even with an experiment. Because many of the individuals assigned to enroll in the program failed to show up, the number of enrollees actually undergoing job training was smaller than the number assigned. The benefits for those enrolling were evidently higher than for those assigned, as table 4.4 shows.

4. These JTPA evaluations examined only the Title II-A programs, not the Title II-C programs, which require local service delivery areas to spend 40 percent of their funding on special youth programs.

5. In addition, these results do not cover the summer youth programs, which provide young people with short-term employment during the summer. There has been little evaluation of these programs, though in general subsidized work experience has not been effective in improving employment of low-income youths (U.S. Department of Labor, 1995, p. 11).

6. The GED, a credential awarded after passage of a multiple-choice test, is intended to be the equivalent of a high school diploma. However, the evidence about its effects is mixed: a careful analysis by Cameron and

Heckman (1993) found that it had no effect on employment once individual differences were controlled, though a recent reanalysis of these data by Murnane, Willett, and Boudett (1995) found positive but still small effects. Other evidence (see Quinn and Haberman, 1986) suggests that earning the GED does not increase the rate at which individuals enroll in postsecondary education.

7. The gains for men and women are substantially smaller than those recorded for CETA, as might be expected given the upward bias of the quasi-experimental results summarized in table 4.2.

8. Welfare payments may fall when individuals earn more, but unless they earn a great deal more they typically remain eligible for welfare. Thus welfare payments can fall without reducing the number of individuals on the welfare rolls.

9. See Lurie and Hagen (1995), for a summary of a large number of monographs on the implementation of JOBS; Grubb and others (1990); and Grubb and McDonnell (1991, 1996).

10. The emphasis on remedial education comes from the fact that individuals in GAIN go through a precise sequence of stages. At an early stage the program evaluates their basic reading and mathematics skills and directs those who are deficient to remedial education. In general, one of the discouraging (but unsurprising) findings of welfare-to-work programs is how many welfare recipients lack basic academic skills.

11. This finding nicely illustrates the amount of movement on and off welfare that occurs naturally, without any special programs: almost half of the single parents in the control group had left welfare by the end of the third year.

12. Across all four programs in table 4.12, the average effect on earnings was 6 percent or about $17 per month ($208 per year).

13. Others have suggested that it is possible to earn the GED with an eighth- or ninth-grade reading level—perhaps an indication why earning a GED has so little influence on either employment or enrollment in postsecondary education.

14. These observations took place in the course of research for Grubb and Kalman (1994). We observed a single program that might not have exemplified the many STEP sites around the country. However, a representative of Public/Private Ventures, the developer of STEP, observed the program with us and assured us that the program we saw was substantially similar to others.

Chapter 5

1. The very preliminary results of the JOBS evaluation have also complicated the simple conclusion that the least job-ready individuals, or those with the greatest barriers to employment, benefit the most. In the labor force attachment approach, those with a high school diploma or GED benefited slightly more than did those without the credential, and mothers with children aged one to five benefited more than did mothers with older children. In contrast, the human capital development approach benefited those without a high school diploma or GED slightly more, with mixed results for mothers with children of different ages (Freedman and Friedlander, 1995, chaps. 2 and 3). However, these results are both premature and statistically insignificant, so it is unwise to make much of them.

2. This is the only comparison that was statistically significant.

3. This is one of the conclusions of Fischer's (1995) and Fischer and Cordray's (1996) meta-analysis of job training programs. However, they provide no numbers to back up this claim and do not include some of the most recent evaluations—the GAIN study by Riccio, Friedlander, and Freedman (1994) and the JTPA study at thirty months by Orr and others (1994), both of which weaken the results—in their analysis.

4. Because the program assigned individuals to services based on which ones were considered appropriate, the characteristics of clients using different services varied and these results are not experimental.

5. I have benefited in writing this section from discussions with Janet Quint and Kay Sherwood. The problems of guidance and counseling arise in similar ways in high schools, community colleges, four-year colleges, job training programs, welfare-to-work programs and other social programs, youth development programs, and programs for the handicapped and the retarded, yet none of these areas of social policy communicates with the others about the issue. I am currently reviewing the literature in these areas to determine what recommendations for good practice are justifiable.

6. This may happen informally; in particular, some individuals claim that locating job training programs in community colleges gives individuals easier access to the educational programs of these institutions (for example, see Grubb and others, 1991). However, my point is that job training programs are not currently structured to lead to subsequent training and education opportunities.

7. In addition to the experimental results reported here, Geraci (1984) used the CLMS to measure the relationship between longer-term earnings and

short-term indicators. In general, the correlations were quite low, indicating the inaccuracy of short-term measures of outcomes.

8. The year 6 employment rates for the Arkansas program are actually extrapolated from two quarters of data, and the year 5 earnings for the Baltimore program, from three quarters of data. These two crucial numbers could therefore be considered less certain than the figures based on four quarters of data even though the method of calculating standard errors, which relies on variation across individuals rather than over time, does not consider this.

9. These results are corroborated by Fischer's (1995) and Fischer and Cordray's (1996) meta-analysis, which concluded that across all studies the mean effect sizes for the proportion employed increase gradually until quarter 10, at the beginning of year 3, but then decay rapidly over the next three quarters. Similarly, the effect sizes for earnings increase until quarter 9 and then decline rapidly; Fischer and Cordray (1996, tables IV-8–IV-11).

10. Bloom and others (1993, exhibit 7.12). This analysis was based on the eighteen-month results, which may be too preliminary, and was not replicated for the thirty-month results.

11. These comments are based not on the published descriptions of the CET program but on several visits by Judy Kalman and the author to CET programs in San Jose and Oakland in the course of research for Grubb and others (1991).

12. Because of its long experience in San Jose, CET may have become a trusted supplier of labor to low-wage employers, who hire through CET rather than through other sources; in this case displacement, or reductions in employment from other sources, might offset the employment effects of CET.

13. The pattern of teaching remedial education and job skills in different and independent segments is typical of job training programs that claim to "integrate" the two; they really mean that they provide both, not that the two are integrated. As in most job training programs, the teaching methods at CET are quite conventional, didactic, and teacher-directed following the practice of "skills and drills."

14. In these cost-benefit analyses, transfer payments are treated correctly; that is, a reduction in welfare benefits is simultaneously a cost to recipients and a benefit to taxpayers, and the overall effect of a transfer on society is zero. The only real saving to society from reducing welfare programs therefore comes from reducing administrative expenses and from the intangible benefits of having fewer individuals rely on welfare.

15. One could argue that the net gains to the government budget and to taxpayers in table 5.10 are so small that they could easily be negative, given random variation in programs.

Chapter 6

1. These conclusions are consistent with Fischer's (1995) and Fischer and Cordray's (1996) meta-analysis. They conclude that effects are significantly different from zero but very small (individuals who receive job training realize average increased earnings of $200–$540 per year and a decrease in welfare payments of $200–$400) and that they generally decay over time. My conclusions are also similar to those of LaLonde (1995). None of these studies says much about why benefits are so low or what should be done next, except for LaLonde's conclusion that only more expensive and intensive services will substantially improve the outcomes. In a way, the conclusions in chapter 7 provide ways of offering more intensive services, not in a framework of job training but within an integrated system that uses the resources of the education system as well.

2. There is even a small amount of evidence for this proposition. In Fischer's (1995) meta-analysis, the effects of job search increased in quarter 2 but decayed essentially to zero in quarter 4, while the effects of basic education programs were initially negative but increased through quarters 2, 3, and 4. In addition, the effects of "staged" job search, in which individuals were screened through job search and proceeded to other activities, including education, also increased, presumably both from screening and human capital effects. See his table B.1.

3. A long-running debate in the United States concerns whether classroom- or work-based training is more effective. The recent infatuation with the work-based apprenticeship systems of Germany and other European countries has led to greater interest in work-based learning even though the pedagogical problems are virtually the same in both settings, as Berryman (1995) has pointed out.

4. For a description of the generally excellent cooperative education programs in Cincinnati, Ohio, that distinguishes those who view cooperative programs as an educational experience from those who view them as a source of well-trained short-term labor, see Villeneuve and Grubb (1996).

5. The issues involved in the skills-and-drills and meaning-making approaches to teaching are complex, since each involves many different assumptions about the nature of learning, the roles of students and teachers, the appropriate competencies to be taught, and the like; for summaries of these differences, see Grubb and others (1991) and Grubb and Kalman (1994).

6. In the course of observing job training and remediation programs, several programs, in particular a Summer Training and Employment Program, almost caused us to violate good research protocol by complaining to senior administrators about the cruel and unusual practices we observed. Even in the highly regarded CET program the teaching was completely conventional.

7. See Grubb and others (1991) and Grubb and Kalman (1994). There are almost surely some exceptions since the job training world is so large and varied; for a very brief description of one of them, in San Diego, see Martinson and Friedlander (1994).

8. Some direct evidence based on learning outcomes points to the superiority of alternatives to conventional teaching for elementary students (Knapp and others, 1995); a meta-analysis of writing has shown that the presentational (or didactic) mode and the conventional teaching of grammar are the least effective approaches (Hillocks, 1986); and some specific practices, like cooperative learning, have been confirmed superior (Slavin, 1987). However, relatively little evidence is based on learning outcomes for adults taught in different ways, partly because relatively little empirical research of any kind has investigated adult education, developmental education in community colleges, and basic skills within job training programs and partly because the efforts to evaluate outcomes of different instructional methods have used inconsistent conceptions of instruction and therefore inconsistent observations of classrooms; see Romberg and Carpenter (1986) for mathematics and Hillocks (1986) for writing. Another problem is that different approaches to teaching generally emphasize different goals: advocates of teaching in the meaning-making tradition usually stress "authentic" tasks and higher-order competencies, which are notoriously difficult to assess reliably, while those following the skills-and-drills approach are more likely to be content with standardized tests.

9. These results are for calendar year 1987. The quality of the data entering these calculations is much poorer than that of the data in random-assignment experiments: the SIPP data are entirely self-reported and are retrospective, generating problems with the accuracy of the reports of having been enrolled in job training. The other independent variables available in the SIPP data are inadequate to control for the various characteristics of those in job training programs; therefore all the coefficients on JTPA and CETA programs are negative, reflecting negative selection.

10. On the problems in the current "system" of education and training, see especially Hansen (1994); Grubb and McDonnell (1991, 1996); McDonnell and Grubb (1991); and Grubb and others (1991, 1992).

11. There are only a few exceptions to the general pattern of job training occurring in isolation from other education and training programs. In some

welfare-to-work programs, caseworkers emphasize "self-initiated placement," in which an individual can put together a series of individualized education and training programs. And some job training programs contract with community colleges to provide short-term job training; in such cases administrators claim as one of the benefits that trainees can easily enroll in regular community college programs (though the frequency of movement from short-term job training to longer-term educational programs in such situations is unknown).

12.   Equivalently, individuals completing job training programs may find employment at the expense of others who do not—though, as mentioned in chapter 3, this displacement cannot be detected with conventional evaluation methods. In economic terms, a shift outward in the supply function for a particular kind of labor (such as for modestly skilled employment) along a stationary and inelastic demand function will result in very little additional employment and in a fall in the wage rate, so placement rates will be low, displacement high, and the increase in earnings modest. In effect, job training programs assume that the demand for labor is relatively elastic.

13.   Because there were only sixteen sites, labor market conditions did not vary much. In addition, the results reflect only the eighteen-month, not the thirty-month, outcomes.

14.   The problem of local political interference is widely acknowledged by observers of job training programs, but almost no one has acknowledged it in writing, probably because of its highly controversial racial dimensions. For an attempt to describe the problem in one community (Fresno, California), see Grubb and McDonnell (1991). Other efforts to cope with this problem have arisen when particular JTPA programs have been investigated for fraud, mismanagement, or ineffectiveness. To my knowledge there has been no analysis of the local politics of job training programs.

15.   In the job training world local programs commonly use a competitive request for proposal (RFP) process whereby the service delivery area invites organizations to bid on proposals for providing services; the competitive RFP process is intended to increase the number of organizations bidding on the basis of low cost and high quality. However, there are numerous ways to manipulate the RFP process to favor certain organizations; for example, RFPs can be written to apply only to specific organizations, or the knowledge that an RFP is rigged for a particular organization will prevent others from applying. RFP and contracting procedures are therefore crucial to local CBOs; one individual commenting on an early draft of this book reported that a charismatic PIC director had his life threatened for changing contracting procedures.

16. For example, in a study of efforts to coordinate job training, welfare-to-work programs, and vocational education, none of the exemplary coordination efforts took place in cities because of the dominance of purely political allocation of resources there; see Grubb and others (1991).

17. See, for example, Traub (1994), who complains about the inappropriateness of providing so much remediation in colleges.

Chapter 7

1. However, it is important not to overstate the value of sub-baccalaureate credentials, since the economic returns vary from field to field and depend critically on placement in related occupations. In addition, the preponderance of the evidence indicates that completion of programs, not simply random course work, enhances earnings. On these issues see Grubb (1995c, 1996).

2. Currently, two-year colleges provide virtually the only links between the two systems: community colleges and technical institutes often provide vocational training for JTPA and welfare clients, and remediation to these individuals as well as their own students. In some areas the community college is the administrator of JTPA programs, and in a few communities it is almost the sole provider of all vocational education, job training, and remediation, coordinating the job training and the education system de facto (Grubb and McDonnell, 1991, 1996). By participating in both job training and education, community colleges already have the potential to move individuals from the short-term job training system into the education system. How often this happens is unclear: even when they administer job training programs, community colleges often establish courses that are independent of the "regular" education programs, and few institutions keep records about the movement of individuals from JTPA (or welfare-to-work programs) into and through certificate and associate degree programs.

3. The historical developments since the 1960s are characterized by an obvious irony: job training programs were developed outside the educational system in part because of the feeling that educational institutions tended to neglect the poor; and federal programs have always been necessary for the poor because states have neglected them. Now consolidation will return control to those very states, and perhaps to the educational institutions, that in the 1960s were thought inadequate to prepare the poor to enter the labor force. One view is that this is simply part of the process of dismantling social programs in general.

4. For a primer recommending practices for summer youth programs that are quite similar to this recommendation, see Center for Human Resources (1993).

5. Within the social services field, the same idea is known as providing a *continuum of services*—for example, a range of mental health programs from highly restrictive, for the most dangerous and worst-off patients, to minimum security facilities and halfway houses, to various forms of counseling and therapy for those able to live on their own. In theory, individuals can enter the continuum at any point appropriate to their needs and progress up and out of the system.

6. JTPA implicitly allows for this possibility by counting either employment or subsequent enrollment as a "successful" termination, but any employment or further education is a success no matter its degree of appropriateness. The creation of ladders would define the most appropriate next steps in education and training.

7. The difference between skill standards and educational credentials is not necessarily large. One way to interpret the movement for skill standards, in which employers together with educators define skills, is that education credentials defined entirely by educators now fail to convey any information about competencies learned. But education credentials need not have these characteristics; an alternative to establishing skill standards independent of educational credentials would be to reform education credentials so that they are competency based and formulated with the participation of employers.

8. I note that this represents yet another manifestation of basing public action on the failure of what would normally be private responsibility; see Grubb and Lazerson (1988). From the larger perspective of social policy, a more effective approach might be to reduce poverty, reduce gender and racial discrimination in employment, and prevent the social pathologies (homelessness, urban decay, crime) that afflict low-income communities. But from the vantage point of education and training programs without the power or resources to make these fundamental changes, providing support services is the best that can be done.

9. The evaluation of the Learning, Earning, and Parenting (LEAP) program for high school dropouts compared students with regular services and students with enhanced services, including neighborhood outreach and enriched GED preparation programs provided by local CBOs. The combination of enhanced services and the incentives embedded in the LEAP program increased the rate at which individuals received a high school diploma or GED from 13.5 percent to 22 percent, a difference of 8.5 percentage points, of which 2 percentage points were attributed to the effects of

the enhanced services themselves (Long, Wood, and Kopp, 1994, table 6.7). (An evaluation of different approaches to support services is now being conducted in Columbus, Ohio, by the Manpower Demonstration Research Corporation, though results will not be available for several years.) Tierney, Grossman, and Resch (1995) have found that mentoring in the Big Brothers/Big Sisters programs generates many positive outcomes. Finally, Reid and others (1994) found that an experimental program providing case management to at-risk adolescent females was more effective than either monetary incentives or no services.

10. On the clients' views of the program see Quint, Musick, and Ladner (1994). On a scale of 0 to 10, the average response to a question about staff caring about clients was 8.0; the average response to a question about case managers providing services was 7.6; see Quint and others (1994), table 3.8. So far, the results of the program are distinctly mixed. The early results indicate that the program increased the rate at which participants stayed in school and completed GEDs and therefore may have been successful in turning young mothers toward future-oriented activities that might provide them more options in both their personal lives and the labor market. However, the effects on earnings, employment, and pregnancy after eighteen months were insubstantial, and large numbers of individuals were clearly derailed from more successful paths by circumstances beyond the control of the program.

11. I note that guidance via an "information dump" is the equivalent of the skills-and-drills approach to instruction, in which content or information is considered paramount regardless of the student's ability to interpret that content.

12. In the past, these funds have included program improvement funds from the Carl Perkins Act, the 6 percent governor's incentive funds, and the 8 percent coordination funds through JTPA. By the time of publication, these federal funds are likely to be consolidated into a new education and training block grant.

References

Ashenfelter, O. 1978. Estimating the effect of training programs on earnings. *Review of Economics and Statistics, LX*(1), 47–57.

Ashenfelter, O., and D. Card. 1985. Using the longitudinal structure of earnings to estimate the effect of training programs. *Review of Economics and Statistics, 7,* 648–660.

Bardach, E. 1993. *Improving the productivity of JOBS programs.* New York: Manpower Demonstration Research Corporation.

Barnow, B. 1986. The impact of CETA programs on earnings: A review of the literature. *Journal of Human Resources, 22,* 157–193.

Bassi, Laurie J. 1983. The effect of CETA on the post-program earnings of participants. *Journal of Human Resources, 18*(4), 539–556.

Bassi, Laurie J., and others. 1984. *Measuring the effect of CETA on youth and the economically disadvantaged.* Final report prepared for the U.S. Department of Labor. Washington: The Urban Institute.

Berryman, S. 1995. Apprenticeship as a paradigm of learning. In W. N. Grubb, ed., *Education through occupations in American high schools. Vol. I. Approaches to integrating academic and vocational education* (pp. 192–214). New York: Teachers College Press.

Bloom, H., and M. McLaughlin. 1982. *CETA training programs: Do they work for adults?* Washington: Congressional Budget Office and National Commission for Employment Policy.

Bloom, H., and others. 1993. *The national JTPA study: Title II-A impacts on earnings and employment at 18 months.* Bethesda, MD: Abt Associates.

Bloom, H. S., and others. 1994. *The national JTPA study: Overview: Impacts, benefits, and costs of Title II-A.* Bethesda, MD: Abt Associates.

Borus, M. E. 1964. A benefit-cost analysis of the economic effectiveness of retraining the unemployed. *Yale Economic Essays, 4*(2), 371–429.

Borus, M. E., and E. C. Prescott. 1974. The effectiveness of MDTA institutional training over time and in periods of high unemployment. In *American Statistical Association, 1973 Proceedings of the Business and Economic Statistics Chapter* (pp. 278–284).

Brazzie, W. F. 1966. Effects of general education in manpower programs. *Journal of Human Resources, 1*(1), 39–44.

Burghardt, J., and A. Gordon. 1990. *More jobs and higher pay: How an integrated program compares with traditional programs.* New York: Rockefeller Foundation.

Burtless, G. 1995. The case for randomized fields trials in economic and policy research. *Journal of Economic Perspectives, 9*(2), 63–84.

Cain, G. G., and E. W. Stromsdorfer. 1968. An economic evaluation of government retraining programs in West Virginia. In G. G. Somers, ed., *Retraining the unemployed* (pp. 299–335). Madison: University of Wisconsin Press.

Cameron, S., and J. Heckman. 1993. The non-equivalence of high school equivalents. *Journal of Labor Economics,11*(1), 1–47.

Cave, G., and others. 1993. *JOBSTART: Final report on a program for school dropouts.* New York: Manpower Demonstration Research Corporation.

Center for Human Resources. 1993. *A primer on improving the quality of academic enrichment in summer youth employment programs.* Waltham, MA: Heller Graduate School, Brandeis University.

Cooley, T. F., T. W. McGuire, and E. C. Prescott. 1975. *The impact of manpower training on earnings: An econometric analysis.* Final report MEL 76-01. Washington: U.S. Department of Labor, Employment and Training Administration, Office of Program Evaluation.

Dickinson, K., T. R. Johnson, and R. W. West. 1984. *An analysis of the impact of CETA programs on participants' earnings.* Final report prepared for the U.S. Department of Labor. Menlo Park, CA: SRI International.

Dickinson, K., D. Kogan, and B. Means. 1994. *JTPA best practices in assessment, case management, and providing appropriate services.* Menlo Park, CA: SRI International and Social Policy Research Associates for the U.S. Department of Labor.

Dickinson, K., and others. 1993. *A guide to well-developed services for dislocated workers.* Menlo Park, CA: SRI International and Social Policy Research Associates for the U.S. Department of Labor.

Dickinson, N. 1986. Which welfare work strategies work? *Social Work, 31*(4), 266–272.

Doolittle, F. No date. Second-chance programs for youth. Unpublished manuscript. Manpower Demonstration Research Corporation.

Doolittle, F., and others. 1993. *A summary of the design and implementation of the national JTPA study.* San Francisco: Manpower Demonstration Research Corporation.

Fischer, R. 1995. Job training as a means to "ending welfare as we know it": A meta-analysis of U.S. welfare employment program effects. Unpublished manuscript. Vanderbilt University.

Fischer, R., and D. Cordray. 1996. *Job training and welfare reform: A policy-driven synthesis.* New York: Russell Sage Foundation (forthcoming).

Fraker, T., and R. Maynard. 1987. The adequacy of comparison group designs for evaluations of employment-related programs. *Journal of Human Resources, 22*(2), 194–227.

Freedman, S., and D. Friedlander. 1995. *The JOBS evaluation: Early findings on program impacts in three sites.* New York: Manpower Demonstration Research Corporation.

Friedlander, D. 1988. *Subgroup impacts and performance indicators for selected welfare employment programs.* New York: Manpower Demonstration Research Corporation.

Friedlander, D., and G. Burtless. 1995. *Five years after: The long-term effects of welfare-to-work programs.* New York: Russell Sage Foundation.

Geraci, V. J. 1984. *Short-term indicators of job training program effects on long-term participant earnings.* Project working paper 2. Austin: University of Texas, Center for Economic Research.

Goldman, B., and others. 1985. *California: Findings from the San Diego demonstration.* New York: Manpower Demonstration Research Corporation.

Gooding, E. C. 1962. *The Massachusetts retraining program, statistical supplement.* Boston: Federal Reserve Bank of Boston.

Gordon, A., and J. Burghardt. 1990. *The minority female single parent demonstration: Short-term economic impacts.* Princeton, NJ: Mathematica Policy Research, Inc.

Gowen, S. 1993. *The politics of workplace literacy.* New York: Teachers College Press.

Granger, R. C. 1994. The policy implications of recent findings from the New Chance Demonstration, Ohio's Learning, Earning, and Parenting (LEAP) program in Cleveland, and the Teenage Parent Demonstration (TPD). Paper presented at the annual meeting of the Association for Public Policy and Management, Chicago, IL.

Grossman, J. B., and C. L. Sipe. 1992. *Summer training and education program (STEP): Report on long-term impacts.* Philadelphia: Public/Private Ventures.

Grubb, W. N., ed. 1995a. *Education through occupations in American high schools. Vol. 1. Approaches to integrating academic and vocational education. Vol. 2. The challenges of implementing curriculum integration.* New York: Teachers College Press.

Grubb, W. N. 1995b. *Evaluating job training programs in the United States: Evidence and explanations.*Training policy study no. 17. Geneva: International Labour Office, Training Policy and Programme Development Branch.

Grubb, W. N. 1995c. *The returns to education and training in the sub-baccalaureate labor market: Evidence from the Survey of Income and Program Participation, 1984–1990.* Berkeley: University of California at Berkeley, National Center for Research in Vocational Education.

Grubb, W. N. 1996. *Working in the middle: Strengthening education and training for the mid-skilled labor force.* San Francisco: Jossey-Bass.

Grubb, W. N., and N. Badway. 1995. Linking school-based and work-based learning: The implications of LaGuardia's co-op seminars for school to-work programs. Prepared for the U.S. Congress, Office of Technology Assessment.

Grubb, W. N., and J. Kalman. 1994. Relearning to earn: The role of remediation in vocational education and job training. *American Journal of Education,* *103*(1), 54–93.

Grubb, W. N., and M. Lazerson. 1988. *Broken promises: How Americans fail their children* (rev. ed.). Chicago: University of Chicago Press.

Grubb, W. N., and L. M. McDonnell. 1991. *Local systems of vocational education and job training: Diversity, interdependence, and effectiveness.* Santa Monica and Berkeley: RAND and the University of California at Berkeley, National Center for Research in Vocational Education.

Grubb, W. N., and L. McDonnell. 1996. Combatting program fragmentation: Local systems of vocational education and job training. *Journal of Policy Analysis and Management, 15*(2).

Grubb, W. N., and R. Wilson. 1992. The effects of demographic and labor market trends on wage and salary inequality, 1967-1988. *Monthly Labor Review* (June), 23–39.

Grubb, W. N., and others. 1989. *Innovation versus turf: Coordination between vocational education and Job Training Partnership Act programs.* Berkeley: University of California at Berkeley, National Center for Research in Vocational Education.

Grubb, W. N., and others. 1990. *Order amidst complexity: The status of coordination among vocational education, Job Training Partnership Act, and welfare-to-work programs.* Berkeley: University of California at Berkeley, National Center for Research in Vocational Education.

Grubb, W. N., and others. 1991. *Readin', writin', and 'rithmetic one more time: The role of remediation in vocational education and job training programs.* Berkeley: University of California at Berkeley, National Center for Research in Vocational Education.

Grubb, W. N., and others. 1992. *Betwixt and between: Education, skills, and employment in the sub-baccalaureate labor market.* Berkeley: University of California at Berkeley, National Center for Research in Vocational Education.

Gueron, J. M. 1987. *Reforming welfare with work.* Ford Foundation Project on Social Welfare and American Future, Occasional paper no. 2. New York: Ford Foundation.

Gueron, J. M., and E. Pauly. 1991. *From welfare to work.* New York: Russell Sage Foundation.

Hansen, J. S., ed. 1994. *Preparing for the workplace: Charting a course for federal postsecondary training policy.* Washington: National Academy Press.

Hardin, E., and M. E. Borus. 1971. *The economic benefits and costs of retraining.* Lexington, MA: D. C. Heath.

Harrison, B., M. Weiss, and J. Gant. 1994. *Building bridges: Community development corporations and the world of employment training.* New York: Ford Foundation.

Heckman, J. 1993. The case for simple estimators: Experimental evidences from the national JTPA study. Technical report 5. Chicago, IL: University of Chicago, Harris School, Center for Social Program Evaluation.

Heckman, J., and J. Smith. 1993. Assessing the case for randomized evaluation of social programs. In K. Jensen and P. K. Madsen (eds.), *Measuring labor market outcomes.* Copenhagen: Ministry of Labor.

Heckman, J., and J. Smith. 1995. Assessing the case for social experiments. *Journal of Economic Perspectives, 9*(2), 85–110.

Hillocks, G. 1986. *Research on written composition: New directions for teaching.* Urbana, IL: ERIC Clearinghouse on Reading and Communications Skills and National Conference on Research in English.

Hull, G. 1993. Critical literacy and beyond: Lessons learned from students and workers in a vocational program and on the job. *Anthropology and Education Quarterly, 24*(4), 373–396.

Kagan, S. L., and others. 1995. *Toward systemic reform: Service integration for young children and their families.* Falls Church, VA: National Center for Service Integration.

Kalman, J., and K. Losey. 1996. Pedagogical innovation in a workplace literacy program: Theory and practice. In G. Hull (ed.), *What workers need to know: Critical looks at literacy, language, and skills in the classroom and on the shop floor.* Albany, NY: SUNY Press (forthcoming).

Kemple, J., D. Friedlander, and V. Fellerath. 1995. *Florida's Project Independence: Benefits, costs, and two-year impacts of Florida's JOBS program.* New York: Manpower Demonstration Research Corporation.

Ketron, Inc. 1979. *The long-term impact of WIN II: A longitudinal evaluation of the employment experiences of participants in the Work Incentive program.* Draft report. Wayne, PA: U.S. Department of Labor, Employment and Training Administration.

Kiefer, N. M. 1976. *The economic benefits from manpower training programs.* Final report. Princeton, NJ: U.S. Department of Labor, Assistant Secretary for Policy and Evaluation Research.

Klerman, J., and L. Karoly. 1994. Young men and the transition to stable employment. *Monthly Labor Review* (August), 31–48.

Knapp, M., and others. 1995. *Teaching for meaning in high-poverty classrooms.* New York: Teachers College Press.

Kogan, D., and others. 1989. *Improving the quality of training under JTPA.* Berkeley: Planning Associates and SRI International for the U.S. Department of Labor.

Kosterlitz, J. 1989. Devil in the details. *National Journal, 21*(48), 2942–2946.

LaLonde, R. 1995. The promise of public sector sponsored training programs. *Journal of Economic Perspectives, 9*(2), 149–168.

Levy, F., and R. Murnane. 1992. U.S. earnings levels and earnings inequality:

A review of recent trends and proposed explanations. *Journal of Economic Literature, 30*(3), 1333–1381.

Lewis, A., and others. 1995. *School-linked comprehensive services for children and families: What we know and what we need to know.* Washington: U.S. Department of Education, Office of Educational Research and Improvement.

Long, D. A., C. D. Mallar, and C. V. D. Thornton. 1981. Evaluating the benefits and costs of the Job Corps. *Journal of Policy Analysis and Management, 1*(1), 55–76.

Long, D., R. Wood, and H. Kopp. 1994. *The educational effects of LEAP and enhanced services in Cleveland.* New York: Manpower Demonstration Research Corporation.

Lurie, I., and J. L. Hagen. 1995. Implementing the JOBS Program: An assessment in ten states. Unpublished manuscript. Albany, NY: Nelson A. Rockefeller Institute of Government, State University of New York.

Main, E. D. 1968. A nationwide evaluation of MDTA institutional job training. *Journal of Human Resources, 3*(2), 159–170.

Mallar, C. 1978. *Evaluation of the economic impact of the Job Corps program: First follow-up report.* Report MEL 79-04. Prepared for the U.S. Department of Labor, Employment and Training Administration, Office of Program Evaluation. Princeton, NJ: Mathematica Policy Research, Inc.

Mallar, C., and others. 1980. *An evaluation of the economic impact of the Job Corps program.* Project report 80-06. Princeton, NJ: Mathematica Policy Research, Inc.

Martinson, K., and D. Friedlander. 1994. *GAIN: Basic education in a welfare-to-work program.* New York: Manpower Demonstration Research Corporation.

McDonnell, L. M., and W. N. Grubb. 1991. *Education and training for work: The policy instruments and the institutions.* R-4026-NCRVE/UCB. Santa Monica, CA: RAND.

McDonnell, L. M., and G. L. Zellman. 1993. *Education and training for work in the fifty states: A compendium of state policies.* N-3560-NCRVE/UCB. Berkeley: University of California, National Center for Research in Vocational Education.

Mecartney, C., M. Styles, and K. Morrow. 1994. *Mentoring in the juvenile justice system: Findings from two pilot studies.* Philadelphia: Public/Private Ventures.

Morrow, K., and M. Styles. 1995. *Building relationships with youth in program settings: A study of Big Brothers/Big Sisters.* Philadelphia: Public/Private Ventures.

Murnane, R., J. Willett, and K. P. Boudett. 1995. Do high school dropouts benefit from obtaining a GED? *Educational Evaluation and Policy Analysis, 17*(2), 133–148.

National Academy of Sciences. 1975. *Knowledge and power in manpower.* Washington: National Academy of Sciences, National Research Council.

National Commission for Employment Policy. 1995. *Understanding federal training and employment programs.* Washington: NCEP.

Nightingale, D. S., and others. 1991. *Evaluation of the Massachusetts employment and training (ET) program.* Urban Institute report 91-1. Washington: Urban Institute Press.

Orr, L. L., and others. 1994. *The national JTPA study: Impacts, benefits, and costs of Title II-A.* Bethesda, MD: Abt Associates.

Page, D. A. 1964. Retraining under the Manpower Development Act: A cost-benefit analysis. In J. D. Montgomery and A. Smithies (eds.), *Public Policy 13* (pp. 257–276). Cambridge, MA: Harvard University.

Palmer, J. 1990. *Accountability through student tracking: A review of the literature.* Washington: American Association of Community and Junior Colleges.

Peterson, G., and others. 1986. *The Reagan block grants: What have we learned?* Washington: Urban Institute.

Prescott, E. C., and T. F. Cooley. 1972. *Evaluating the impact of MDTA programs on earnings under varying labor market conditions.* Final report MEL 73-08. Philadelphia: U.S. Department of Labor, Employment and Training Administration, Office of Policy, Evaluation and Research.

Quinn, L., and M. Haberman. 1986. Are GED certificate holders ready for post-secondary education? *Metropolitan Education* (Fall), 72–82.

Quint, J. C., J. S. Musick, and J. A. Ladner. 1994. *Lives of promise, lives of pain.* New York and San Francisco: Manpower Demonstration Research Corporation.

Quint, J. C., and others. 1994. *New Chance: Interim findings on a comprehensive program for disadvantaged young mothers and their children.* San Francisco: Manpower Demonstration Research Corporation.

Rangarajan, A., J. Burghardt, and A. Gordon. 1992. *Evaluation of the Minority Female Single Parent Demonstration. Vol. 2. Technical supplement to the analysis of economic impacts.* Princeton, NJ: Mathematica Policy Research, Inc.

Reid, W., and others. 1994. Cash incentives vs. case management: Can money replace services in preventing school failure? *Social Work Research, 18*(4).

Riccio, J., D. Friedlander, and S. Freedman. 1994. *GAIN: Benefits, costs, and three-year impacts of a welfare-to-work program.* San Francisco: Manpower Demonstration Research Corporation.

Rockefeller Foundation and Wider Opportunities for Women. 1989. *Literacy and the Marketplace: Improving the literacy of low-income single mothers.* New York: Rockefeller Foundation.

Romberg, T., and T. Carpenter. 1986. Research on teaching and learning mathematics: Two disciplines of scientific inquiry. In M. C. Wittrock (ed.), *Handbook of research on teaching* (3d ed.) (pp. 850–873). New York: Macmillan.

Roomkin, M. 1973. The benefits and costs of basic education for adults: A case study. In *Benefit-cost analysis of federal programs* (pp. 211–223). Submitted to the Subcommittee on Priorities and Economy in Government of the Joint Economic Committee, 92nd Cong., 2nd sess. Washington: U.S. Government Printing Office.

Roueche, J. E., and G. A. Baker III. 1987. *Access and excellence: The open door college.* Washington: The Community College Press.

Rumberger, R., and T. Daymont. 1984. The economic value of academic and vocational training acquired in high school. In Michael Borus (ed.), *Youth and the labor market: Analyses of the National Longitudinal Survey.* Kalamazoo, MI: W. E. Upjohn Institute for Employment Research.

Sewell, D. O. 1971. *Training the poor.* Kingston, Ontario: Queen's University, Industrial Relations Centre.

Slavin, R. 1987. Cooperative learning and the cooperative school. *Educational Leadership* (November), 7–13.

State of California. 1976. *Third year and final report on the community work experience program.* Sacramento: State of California, Employment Development Department.

Taggart, R. 1981. *A fisherman's guide: An assessment of training and remediation strategies.* Kalamazoo, MI: W. E. Upjohn Institute.

Tierney, J., J. Grossman, and N. Resch. 1995. *Making a difference: An impact study of Big Brothers/Big Sisters.* Philadelphia: Public/Private Ventures.

Traub, J. 1994. Class struggle. *New Yorker,* September 19, 1994, 76–90.

U.S. Department of Labor. 1995. *What's working (and what's not): A summary of research on the economic impacts of employment and training programs.* Washington: U.S. Department of Labor, Office of the Chief Economist.

U.S. General Accounting Office. 1987. *Work and welfare: Current AFDC work programs and implications for federal policy.* Washington: U.S. General Accounting Office.

U.S. General Accounting Office. 1995a. *Job Corps: High costs and mixed results raise questions about program's effectiveness.* GAO/HEHS-95-180. Washington: U.S. General Accounting Office.

U.S. General Accounting Office. 1995b. *Multiple employment training programs: Major overhaul needed to create a more efficient, customer-driven system.* Washington: U.S. General Accounting Office.

Villeneuve, J., and W. N. Grubb. 1996. *Indigenous school-to-work programs: Lessons from Cincinnati's co-op education.* Berkeley: University of California at Berkeley, National Center for Research in Vocational Education (forthcoming).

Walker, G., and F. Vilella-Velez. 1992. *Anatomy of a demonstration: The Summer Training and Education Program (STEP) from pilot through replication and post-program impacts.* Philadelphia: Public/Private Ventures.

Weil, M., J. Karls, and Associates. 1985. *Case management in human service practice.* San Francisco: Jossey-Bass.

Weisberg, A. 1988. *Computers, basic skills, and job training programs: Advice for policymakers and practitioners.* New York: Manpower Demonstration Research Corporation.

Westat, Inc. 1981. *Continuous longitudinal manpower survey new impact report no. 1: Impact on 1977 earnings of new FY 1976 CETA enrollees in selected program activities.* Report prepared for the U.S. Department of Labor. Bethesda, MD: Westat Inc.

Westat, Inc. 1984. *Summary of net impact results.* Report prepared for the U.S. Department of Labor. Bethesda, MD: Westat Inc.

Zambrowski, A., and A. Gordon. 1993. *Evaluation of the minority female single parent demonstration: Fifth year impact at CET.* Princeton, NJ: Mathematica Policy Research, Inc.

Index

Boldface numbers refer to tables and figures.